Belle Boyd, Sam Wylde Hardinge

Belle Boyd

In Camp and Prison. Vol. 2

Belle Boyd, Sam Wylde Hardinge

Belle Boyd
In Camp and Prison. Vol. 2

ISBN/EAN: 9783744759410

Printed in Europe, USA, Canada, Australia, Japan

Cover: Foto ©ninafisch / pixelio.de

More available books at **www.hansebooks.com**

BELLE BOYD,

IN

CAMP AND PRISON.

With an Introduction

BY A FRIEND OF THE SOUTH.

IN TWO VOLUMES.

VOL. II.

LONDON:
SAUNDERS, OTLEY, AND CO.,
66 BROOK STREET, W.
1865.

CONTENTS

OF VOLUME THE SECOND.

CHAPTER I.

PAGE

I leave for Fortress Monroe—I am not permitted to see my Father—Interview with General Butler—My Luggage undergoes an Examination—Much of my Property is confiscated—General Jackson's Field-glasses—My Letters of Introduction almost get me into Trouble—Kindness of Major Mulford and his Wife—General Butler attempts to re-capture me—

The bird is flown, and to his chagrin, as I afterwards learn—Ascending the James River The French Corvette—The Mirage—Arrival in Richmond 1

CHAPTER II.

Kind reception at Richmond—I hear of my Father's Death—Efforts of my Friends to procure my Return Home—I go from Richmond further south—Kindness of friends during my illness—I am made Bearer of Despatches—Departure from Richmond—Too late for the *Coquette*—I take passage in the *Greyhound* . . . 20

CHAPTER III.

I leave Wilmington for Europe — Running the Blockade — Safe outside—*Mal de mer* — The Federal Cruiser — The Chase — The Yankee proves too fast—The First Shell—The Fire grows hot—Forced to surrender—The English Sailor and his Flag 31

CHAPTER IV.

We are boarded by an Officer from the Yankee—The U.S. Steamer *Connecticut*—An Officer, but no Gentleman—Strange state of Yankee Discipline—Scenes on Board of the *Greyhound* after her Capture—"Ain't ye skeared?"—A proud boast 44

CHAPTER V.

An eventful Meeting—A Gentleman at last—A Wife's Apology—Mr. Hardinge—I am disappointed—A pleasant Exchange—Farewell to Mr. Swasey—A ludicrous Incident—Captain "Henry's" best Boots—I am discovered through Treachery 52

CHAPTER VI.

Bound North—We are taken in tow—Our first Evening at Sea—We arrive at Fortress Monroe—Commodore Guerte Gansevoorte comes on Board in James River—We are paroled by him—His indignation against Mr. Hardinge for flying the English Ensign—The Commodore's Conduct whilst on Board—Arrival at New York—We go on Shore—I visit Niblos' Theatre—Return aboard and Departure for Boston—Love triumphant! . 62

CHAPTER VII.

Arrival in Boston — Our plan for re-capturing the *Greyhound* frustrated—Captain "Henry's"

Escape — How it was managed — Marshal Keyes comes on Board—The Search for the Captain — A false Report of his Arrest — I communicate with him—He leaves for New York—I bid adieu to the *Greyhound*—My Quarters on Shore — I am paroled for the City — Newspaper Rumours — Mr. Hardinge proceeds to Washington in my behalf—My Mother telegraphs to the Marshal—She is not permitted to see me—Politeness of the British Consul—I write a Letter to the Secretary of the Navy — Am pronounced insane — I am liberated—Mr. Hardinge and his Officers are placed under Arrest—Mr. Pollard is sent to Fort Warren—I leave for Canada . . . 84

CHAPTER VIII.

Arrival at Montreal — Niagara — A System of Espionage still around me — I depart for Europe—Passage across the Atlantic—Arrival in London—I meet Mr. Hardinge once more —Our Marriage—Comments of the Press . 102

CHAPTER IX.

Lieutenant Hardinge's Journal—Arrival at Home—A Surprise—A silent Breakfast—Visit to Martinsburg—A pleasant little Excitement—A Negro Welcome—"Miss Belle's Husband"—A Portent—A Sailor's superstition—Capture—Poor Pat in the toils—A high-bred General—Lieutenant Adams—A Yankee Provost-Marshal—The Guard-house—The Restaurant—A Guardsman—Ordered off again—Arrival at Washington . . 117

CHAPTER X.

Forrest Hall—A Lesson on Prison Luxury—The Torture—Close Packing—The "Neutral

Ground "—A good-natured Sentry—An Aristocrat — The Gouger — A tough Contest—Homage to the Victor—An Honour declined—The Carroll Prison—Defacing the Walls—Piety Hall — Unpleasant Tortures — "The Colonel" 137

CHAPTER XI.

Journal continued—Letter to Mr. Stanton—Visit from Judge Turner — Room 25 — An Introduction in due form—Pleasant Society — A Dinner at last—Good Advice—A clandestine Communication—False Alarm—"That reminds me of a good Story "—A Massachusetts Officer in Trouble — The " Smasher's " Sentence—An imprisoned Wife and Child—Blockade-running 158

CHAPTER XII.

Introduced to the Ladies' Ward—Colonel Wood and his "Reminiscence-book" — Interview with Judge Turner — Sherman's Officers in Georgia—A hideous Outrage—Christmas in Prison — Home-sick — A drunken Sentry—Another Visit to the Ladies — The Young Girl's Sick Bed—A Rough Prison Carol . 172

CHAPTER XIII.

Mr. H.'s Journal continued—A Visit from my Parents—The Order for Removal—On the March—"Do you know Belle Boyd?"—An abrupt Introduction—Arrival in Philadelphia—Dismal Night Quarters — An unpleasant Ordeal—The Menagerie—*En route* for Wilmington—An Eight-mile March—The *Osceola*—Fort Delaware — "Fresh Fish" — "Miss

Belle Boyd's Husband"—New Year's Eve—
Turned Cook—Snow-balling—Sharp Practice 190

CHAPTER XIV.

The "Pens"—Officers' Barracks—Privates' Barracks—The "Galvanized" Barracks—Galvanization and its results—General T.'s Experiment—The Barracks by Night—A Reckless Sentry—The wrong Man shot . . . 210

CHAPTER XV.

A piteous Spectacle—The Old Men's Petition—Piety of the Southern Soldiery—A Young Men's Christian Association—A Prison Service—Our Guardians—Colonel Wood—Mr. Wilson—Tom S. the Toady—How Tom got his Situation—The Ladies' Attendants—Aunt Lizzie—Mr.

L.—The Spy discomfited — Our Cuisine — Scrap Pudding—How the Prison Officers made their Profit 219

CHAPTER XVI.

Miss McDonough—A brutal Outrage—Treatment of Mr. W. R. Coyner—The "Court-martial"—Sentence—"Tossing in a Blanket"—The Torture by Fire—Fort Delaware—A Box of Clothing—A Man of Consequence—Adjutant and General — The Blankets at last—The "Softest Plank" 242

CHAPTER XVII.

Wanted at the Fort—The Order for Release—Farewells — Free at last — A cool Reception — An undignified Costume — No Conveyance—The Walk to Wilmington—Home

once more — Conclusion of Mr. Hardinge's
Journal 258

CHAPTER XVIII.

Conclusion of Mrs. S. Hardinge's Narrative . . 269

BELLE BOYD.

CHAPTER I.

I leave for Fortress Monroe—I am not permitted to see my Father—Interview with General Butler—My Luggage undergoes an examination—Much of my Property is confiscated—General Jackson's Field-glasses—My Letters of Introduction almost get me into Trouble—Kindness of Major Mulford and his Wife—General Butler attempts to re-capture me—The bird is flown, and to his chagrin, as I afterwards learn—Ascending the James River—The French Corvette—The Mirage—Arrival in Richmond.

On the first day of December, early in the

morning, I started for Fortress Monroe, under the charge of Captain Mix and an orderly-sergeant. It was my poor father's intention to have accompanied me as far as Baltimore, and beyond, if he could get the necessary permission. Just before I left, however, a message was brought to me stating that my father, though not dangerously ill, was confined to the house by severe indisposition.

When I heard that I could not see my fond parent, it distressed me greatly; but I was powerless to act in the matter; and, though I entreated them to let me go to him, if but for a moment, it was refused.

After being subjected to the annoying and ungentlemanly conduct of Captain Mix, who seemed to exert himself especially to make everything as disagreeable as he possibly could for me, I arrived in Fortress Monroe about 9 a.m. on Wednesday morning. Captain Mix immediately went on shore to report to Captain Cassels, the Provost-Marshal and aide-de-camp to Butler, to whose care I was to be committed until the "exchange boat" should start for Richmond.

Meanwhile all the passengers had landed, and I was left in the charge of the orderly-sergeant. Major (now General) Mulford, the exchange officer, returned on board with Captain Mix, and was introduced to me. I found him an elegant and courteous gentleman. In a short time I was escorted from the boat to the Provost-Marshal's office, passing between a company of negro soldiers, who were filed on each side. Thence I was taken into the fortress, to Butler's head-quarters, and, after waiting a short time, I was conducted into his august presence.

He was seated near a table, and, upon my entrance, he looked up and said, "Ah, so this is Miss Boyd, the famous rebel spy. Pray be seated."

"Thank you, General Butler, but I prefer to stand."

I was very much agitated, and trembled greatly. This he noticed, and remarked, "Pray be seated. But why do you tremble so? Are you frightened?"

"No; ah! that is, yes, General Butler; I must acknowledge that I do feel frightened in the presence of a man of such world-wide reputation as yourself."

This seemed to please him immensely, and, rubbing his hands together and smiling most benignly, he said, "Oh, pray do be seated, Miss Boyd. But what do you mean when you say that I am widely known?"

"I mean, General Butler," I said, "that you are a man whose atrocious conduct and brutality, especially to Southern ladies, is so infamous that even the English Parliament commented upon it. I naturally feel alarmed at being in your presence."

He had evidently expected a compliment when I commenced to reply to his inquiry, but, at the close of my remarks, he rose, and, with rage depicted upon every lineament of his features, he ordered me out of his presence.

I was conducted to the hotel, and felt for the time being exceedingly uneasy lest by my Parthian shot at an enemy whom I thoroughly detested, I should have laid myself open to his petty spirit of revenge. I feared that I should be remanded to a dreary prison cell; for General Butler was all-powerful in the North about this period.

Events have since clearly proved this man, even to the Yankees themselves, to be but a meretricious hero and a political charlatan. Like others who render themselves rather notorious than great, he first pleased a fickle populace by his acts of brutality, then disgusted his contemporaries, who feared that he might become to America what Robespierre had been to France. The tyrant of New Orleans, having failed most signally at Wilmington, was discovered to be a coward, and suspected of being a rogue. Well might the baffled New England attorney exclaim, "*Facilis descensus Averni!*" In the hope of being styled a modern Cincinnatus, he retired to Lowell, to live upon the ill-gotten gains extorted by threats or force from Southern people.

But to resume the thread of my story. I was obliged to give my parole that I would not leave the house until permitted to do so. Here I found the Misses Lomax, sisters of the Confederate General Lomax, and a Miss Goldsborough, of Baltimore, who were to be sent south. These ladies, however, were not the only Confederate sympathizers in the hotel; there were others whose names I dare not mention.

On Wednesday evening the order came for Miss Goldsborough and myself to be in readiness to start that same night for Richmond. The Misses Lomax, for some reason, were not allowed to proceed, but were sent back to Baltimore. When the time arrived for our departure, we were taken back to the Provost-Marshal's office; and here I found my luggage, consisting of two Saratoga trunks and a bonnet-box. The keys were demanded of me, and I complied with the request.

A man and two women immediately set to work to ransack my boxes, although I assured them that they need not search, as I had just come from prison. This appeal, however, was ineffectual, and they still continued their examination. Imagine their astonishment and my chagrin when they pulled from the bottom of one of my trunks two suits of private clothes, a uniform for Major-General W——, a dozen linen shirts, &c. These things I had succeeded in smuggling into prison by means of an underground railway, of which Superintendent Wood, sharp as he imagined himself to be, was little aware. I was interrogated as to how I had obtained the articles in question, but they did not succeed in eliciting anything by their queries.

All the goods considered contraband, including several pairs of army gauntlets and felt hats, with a pair of field-glasses which had formerly belonged to General Jackson, and which I greatly prized, together with much clothing, were taken from me. I entreated them to let me retain the glasses; but this was flatly refused; and they were, to my mortification, given to General Butler.

When I saw how these Vandals were robbing me of nearly everything, I strove in vain to restrain my tears; and my trunks having been thoroughly ransacked, I was informed that I must undergo a personal search. At this turn of affairs I began to feel very nervous, for I had concealed about me twenty thousand dollars in Confederate notes, five thousand in green-backs, and nearly one thousand in gold, as well as the letters of introduction which I have previously mentioned. I earnestly appealed to their forbearance, assuring them that I had nothing contraband; for I did not consider my money contraband.

As it was getting late, the captain said, "Well, if you will take an oath to the effect that you have nothing contraband upon you—no letters or papers—you shall not be searched."

As this was impossible, I told him that I could not make such a declaration, handing him my letters at the same time. He then asked if I had any money about me. To this I replied by giving him a roll of two or three thousand dollars in Confederate money, which I had placed in my pocket. This he regarded as valueless, and sneeringly informed me that I might keep "that stuff."

Upon opening my letters and finding mention of "my immense services to my country," "my kindness towards prisoners," "my devotion to the Southern cause," &c., he became very angry, and said, "I shall send this to General Butler in the morning. I would do so now, but it is after office hours."

Miss Goldsborough sat by meanwhile, a quiet spectator of the whole affair, she having undergone the ordeal of search in the morning. We were then conducted to the wharf, placed on board a tug, and sent off to the exchange boat, the *City of New York*, which lay at anchor in the stream. Upon our arrival on board we were kindly received by Major Mulford, who conducted us to the saloon and introduced us to his wife, a very charming, lady-like woman. Here we remained all night, and next morning, about seven o'clock, got under way. Shortly afterwards we ran aground, and it was not until 8 a.m. that we succeeded in getting the vessel off again. Then, under a full head of steam, we steered for City Point.

About this time the little steam-tug that had brought us alongside the *City of New York* quitted the wharf, apparently in chase of us. My heart sank, for I felt intuitively that this pursuit had something to do with me, and that General Butler must have given an order for my detention. But the larger steamer had already waited so long that Major Mulford, angry and impatient at the delay, took no notice of our pursuers, and, to my great joy and relief, kept steadily on our course.

I afterwards learnt that my fears upon this occasion were not unfounded. When General Butler, smarting with the remembrance of my farewell sarcasm, had beheld the letters that Captain Cassels had taken from me, he commanded that I should be followed, and, if re-captured, should be sent at once to Fort Warren, in Massachusetts Bay. As he issued this order he remarked to those who surrounded him that he would take "a leading character in 'Beauty and the Beast.'" When the tug returned from her fruitless chase, he was almost beside himself with rage at being thwarted in his revenge. This I had from such good authority that I am confident the General will not feel it worth his while to contradict the statement.

At the mouth of the James River we passed the Federal blockading fleet, and were here boarded by a boat from the flagship *Minnesota*, commanded by Admiral Lee. In a few moments we had entered the James, whose waters are distinguishable from those of the Potomac by a yellow streak which appears on the surface.

As we wended our way up the river we could see the signal-officers at the different stations busily announcing our approach, and occasionally we observed Confederate soldiers on picket duty. Everything reminded me that I was once more drawing near to the capital of my own sunny South.

> "Amate sponde!
> Pur vi torno a riveder,
> Trema in petto e si confonde
> L'alma oppressa dal piacer."

Though exceedingly happy that I was again permitted to breathe the pure air of my native State, I did not feel completely free, for I was still under the Federal flag, and could scarcely count upon my liberty as being yet fully assured to me.

We arrived at City Point late on Friday evening. This place, which could hardly be correctly dignified with the name of village, is situate in a bend of the river. It was used as a dépôt by the Confederates, for the purpose of forwarding stores to those of their unfortunate countrymen who were prisoners in the North.

Whilst the *City of New York* was coming to an anchor, Major Mulford, his wife, Miss Goldsborough, and myself stood conversing on the hurricane-deck. Major Mulford remarked, pointing to what was apparently the Confederate flag-of-truce boat approaching, "After all, ladies, you will not have to remain on board here to-night."

Looking in the direction indicated, we distinctly saw a steamer, which, judging from the distance between us, would in less than ten minutes be alongside. Ten minutes, however, passed in fruitless expectation; then followed twenty more of hope deferred; when Major Mulford, who began to grow very impatient, went on shore to inquire the reason of her remaining as she did—he even sent a boat to her to ascertain the reason of her detention. Major Mulford was so confident that he had seen her that the Confederate officer commanding the "Point" telegraphed the news to Richmond. Judge of our great surprise when the telegraphic reply, brought to us on board shortly afterwards, announced " that the

Confederate flag-of-truce boat had left Richmond exactly at the hour we had seen her." As Richmond was more than twelve hours distant from us at the then rate of travel over that route, we could only consider that we had been deceived by a "mirage." How often must such phenomena have given rise to stories of phantom ships!

A French corvette, which had been up the river to Richmond, lay at anchor near us. This evening, in acceptance of an invitation from Major Mulford, the French captain and his lieutenant came on board to spend the evening with us; and we enjoyed their visit heartily. The next morning, when I awoke, I found that the flag-of-truce boat had arrived during the night. Captain Hatch, the Confederate exchange officer, presently came on board.

We were introduced to him, and very soon afterwards were, with our luggage, safely ensconced in the snug little cabin of the ——. Here, under my own country's flag, I felt free and comparatively happy.

On our way up the river to Richmond we had to pass the obstructions situated between Chapin's and Drury's Bluffs. These places take their names from the bold appearance that the shore here presents. The obstructions designed to impede a hostile squadron became accidentally hurtful to our Confederate vessel. She ran foul of them, and it was found utterly impossible to continue the voyage.

At Drury's Bluff, therefore, we went on board a tug, in which we proceeded to Richmond. When we arrived, at 8 p.m., I went immediately to the Spottswood House, and, tired and worn out with the fatigues of my journey, I retired to rest, refusing to see any one that evening.

CHAPTER II.

Kind reception at Richmond—I hear of my Father's Death—Efforts of my Friends to procure my Return Home—I go from Richmond further south—Kindness of Friends during my Illness—I am made bearer of Despatches—Departure from Richmond —Too late for the *Coquette*—I take passage in the *Greyhound*.

When I came down to breakfast on the following day, my many acquaintances and friends in the hotel were astonished to see me, for few had expected that I should be released, and none that I should so soon arrive at Richmond. The morning papers announced my return in flattering terms; and, as it thus became generally known, I was at once besieged with company, and every afternoon and evening I held a perfect drawing-room, if I may be allowed to make use of the expression. My reception was everything that I could wish; but, alas! my happiness was of short duration, and my freedom was dearly bought.

I was at a large dinner-party on a Saturday evening exactly one week after the day I had arrived. I was joyous and light-hearted, little dreaming of the blow that was to overwhelm me with sadness—little dreaming that I should be so cruelly reminded of the words of the Preacher that " in the midst of life we are in death;" but so it was.

On Monday morning, the 14th, before I had risen, I received a little note from Captain Hatch, in which he expressed great sorrow at having to be the bearer of mournful tidings, and said that, as soon as I was dressed, he would call in person with the wife of the proprietor of the hotel. For one moment I could not imagine what he meant, but, dressing myself as speedily as I possibly could, I sent for them. They came: Captain Hatch held in his hands a newspaper. He approached me, saying—

"Miss Belle, you are aware that you left your father ill?"

In one moment I comprehended everything, and exclaiming "My God! is he dead?" I sank fainting to the floor.

This swoon was succeeded by severe illness; and I felt all the loneliness of my position. An exile (for the Yankees held possession of Martinsburg) and an orphan—these words described me; and ah! how hard they seemed!

One of those strange warnings that are sometimes given to mortals, or that are, some would say, the imaginings of an excited brain shaken by sickness, ought to have prepared me for my sad bereavement.

> "Some say that gleams of a remoter world
> Visit the soul in sleep."

The night upon which my father died I had retired to rest somewhat earlier than usual. How long I slept I do not know, but I suddenly awoke, or seemed to awaken, from my sleep, although I had neither the power nor the wish to move. In the centre of the room I saw General Jackson, whose eyes rested sorrowfully upon me. Beside him stood my father, gazing at me, but saying nothing. I was dumb, or I should have spoken, for I did not feel alarmed. As I looked upon those two standing together, General Jackson turned and spoke to my father. I remember the words distinctly.

"It is time for us to go," he said; and, taking my father's hand, he led him away, adding as he did so, "Poor child!"

I afterwards learnt by a letter from my mother (the first and only communication received from her until my arrival in this country) that my beloved father, at the news of my being sent south, where I should have to battle alone with the world, had grown rapidly worse, and had expired the very next day after my arrival in Richmond. My mother and the children had been sent for, and reached my father just before he died. Although he retained his senses up to the last, he frequently spoke of me, declared that I was hovering around his couch, and would become quite restless if people in the room went to a certain spot near the bed, exclaiming that "I was being torn from him!"

Several of our senators and exchange officers, with many other influential persons, wrote to the Federal Government to try and obtain permission for me to return to my sorrowing mother. I myself wrote to the Northern President and Secretary Stanton, at the suggestion of my friends, and appealed to them as a Mason's daughter. But no, every appeal was refused.

My letters to and from my mother in Martinsburg were intercepted; and from December the 16th until I arrived in London, and then not until the following October, did I receive one line from her, though she had written repeatedly.

My health was very bad and my constitution greatly undermined; so in February I went from Richmond farther south, visiting Mobile, Atalanta, Augusta, and other cities whose names have since become historical.

I cannot express one half the gratitude that I feel to the many kind hosts whom I met in my journey through the South. During my illness in Richmond I was well cared for; and amongst the warmest of my friends must be ranked the wife of the world-renowned Captain Semmes (afterwards Admiral Semmes), of the ill-fated *Alabama.*

Mrs. Semmes treated me with as much attention as though I had been her own daughter, and invited me to visit them at their home in Mobile. I had always been termed " the child of the Confederacy," or " the child of the army;" and, no matter where I went, I was welcomed both by the gentry and the people.

In March I returned to Richmond, when, although somewhat recovered, my health still required care. I could not return home, and I felt, moreover, restless and unhappy at the death of my father. I determined, therefore, to visit Europe so soon as I could arrange my affairs. When I made known this resolution to President Davis, he approved of the plan, considering me to need quiet and rest in some place remote from the dangers of our sorely-pressed country.

Orders were given to the Confederate Secretary of State to make me the bearer of despatches. I commenced preparations for departure as speedily as possible.

The despatches were ready for me on March 25th, but a brief return of illness hindered me from starting, and, as these papers, being very important, could not be delayed, they were forwarded by some other hand.

At last, on March 29th, I was able to leave Richmond, having recovered sufficiently for travelling. Other despatches were now ready, and of them I was made the bearer.

Owing to an accident on the railway,

we did not arrive in Wilmington until several hours after the departure of the blockade-runner in which I was to have sailed.

This steamer would not be followed by another for at least a fortnight, because they did not run out during the brilliant nights of the full moon, lest they should fall an easy prey to Yankee blockaders. I was therefore obliged to await the arrival and departure of the next regular steamer, as, even putting aside all consideration of difficulties increased by moonlight, there was not a suitable craft in port.

One of the first vessels that arrived was the *Greyhound*, commanded by Captain " Henry," formerly, it is said, an officer in the United States navy, and who had, at the commencement of the war, with many of his comrades, sent in his resignation to the United States Navy Department, and entered the Confederate service. Captain "Henry" had formerly been on "Stonewall" Jackson's staff; and, as I was acquainted with his family, I gladly accepted his kind invitation, and took passage on board the *Greyhound*, feeling doubly secure under such a skilful commander.

CHAPTER III.

I leave Wilmington for Europe—Running the Blockade—Safe outside—*Mal de mer*—The Federal Cruiser—The Chase—The Yankee proves too fast—The first Shell—The Fire grows hot—Forced to surrender—The English Sailor and his Flag.

On the 8th of May I bade farewell to many friends in Wilmington and stepped on board the *Greyhound*. It was, as may well be imagined, an anxious moment. I knew that the venture was a desperate one; but I felt sustained by the greatness of my cause; for I had borne a part, however insignificant, in one of the greatest dramas ever yet enacted upon the stage of the world; moreover, I relied upon my own resources, and I looked to Fortune, who is so often the handmaid of a daring enterprise.

At the mouth of the river we dropped anchor, and decided to wait until the already waning moon should entirely disappear.

Outside the bar, and at the distance of about six miles, lay the Federal fleet, most of them at anchor; but some of their lighter vessels were cruising quietly in different directions. Not one, however, showed any disposition to tempt the guns of the fort over which the Confederate flag was flying.

There were on board the *Greyhound* two

passengers, or rather adventurers, besides myself—Mr. Newell and Mr. Pollard, the latter the editor of the "Richmond Examiner." We laughed and joked, as people will laugh and joke in the face of imminent danger, and even in the jaws of death.

Gentle reader, before you accuse us of levity, or of a reckless spirit of fatalism, reflect how, in the prison of La Force, when the reign of terror was at its height, the doomed victims of the guillotine acted charades, played games of forfeits, and circulated their *bon mots* and *jeux d'esprit* within a few hours of a violent death. Remember also that the lovely Queen of Scots and the unfortunate Anne Boleyn met their fate with a smile, and greeted the scaffold with a jest.

About ten o'clock orders were given to

get under way. The next minute every light was extinguished, the anchor was weighed, steam was got up rapidly and silently, and we glided off just as "the trailing garments of the night" spread their last folds over the ocean.

The decks were piled with bales of cotton, upon which our look-out men were stationed, straining their eyes to pierce the darkness and give timely notice of the approach of an enemy.

I freely confess that our jocose temperament had now yielded to a far more serious state of feeling. No more pleasantries were exchanged, but many earnest prayers were breathed. No one thought of sleep. Few words were spoken. It was a night never to be forgotten—a night of silent, almost breathless, anxiety. It seemed to us as if day would never break;

but it came at last, and, to our unspeakable joy, not a sail was in sight. We were moving unmolested and alone upon a tranquil sea, and we indulged in the fond hope that we had eluded our eager foes.

Steaming on, we ran close by the wreck of the Confederate iron-clad *Raleigh*, which had so lately driven the Federal blockading squadron out to sea, but which now lay on a shoal, an utter wreck, parted amidships, destroyed, not by the Federals, but by a visitation of Providence.

At this point we three passengers began to experience those sensations which, although invariably an object of derision to persons who are exempt from them, are, for the time being, as grievous to the sufferer as any in the whole catalogue of pains and aches to which flesh is heir.

Reader, may it never be your lot, as it then was mine, to find sea-sickness overcome by the stronger emotion inspired by the sight of a hostile vessel bearing rapidly down with the purpose of depriving you of your freedom.

It was just noon, when a thick haze which had lain upon the water lifted, and at that moment we heard a startled cry of "Sail ho!" from the look-out man at the mast-head. These ominous words were the signal for a general rush aft. Extra steam was got up in an incredibly short space of time, and sail was set with the view both of increasing our speed and of steadying our vessel as she dashed through the water.

Alas! it was soon evident that our exertions were useless, for every minute visibly lessened the distance between us and our pursuer; her masts rose higher and higher, her hull loomed larger and larger, and I was told plainly that, unless some unforeseen accident should favour us, such as a temporary derangement of the Federal steamer's steering apparatus, or a breaking of some important portion of her machinery, we might look to New York instead of Bermuda as our destination.

My feelings at this intelligence must be imagined: I can describe them but inadequately. "Unless," I thought, "Providence interposes directly in our behalf, we shall be overhauled and captured; and then what follows? I shall suffer a third rigorous imprisonment." Moreover, I was the bearer of despatches from my Government to authorities in Europe; and I knew that this service, honourable and necessary as it was, the Federals regarded in the light of a heinous crime, and that, in all probability, I should be subjected to every kind of indignity.

The chase continued, and the cruiser still gained upon us. For minutes, which to me seemed hours, did I strain my eyes towards our pursuer and watch anxiously for the flash of the gun that would soon send a shot or shell after us, or, for all I could tell, into us. How long I remained watching I know not, but the iron messenger of death came at last. A thin white curl of smoke rose high in the air as the enemy luffed up and presented her formidable broadside. Almost simultaneously with the hissing sound of the shell, as it buried itself in the sea within a few yards of us, came the smothered report of its explosion under water.

The enemy's shots now followed each other in rapid succession: some fell very close, while others, less skilfully aimed, were wide of the mark, and burst high in the air over our heads. During this time bale after bale of cotton had been rolled overboard by our crew, the epitaph of each as it disappeared beneath the waves being "By ——! there's another they shall not get."

Our captain paced nervously to and fro, now watching the compass, now gazing fixedly at the approaching enemy, now shouting "More steam! more steam! give her more steam!" At last he turned suddenly round to me, and exclaimed in passionate accents—

"Miss Belle, I declare to you that, but for your presence on board, I would burn her to the water's edge rather than those infernal scoundrels should reap the benefit of a single bale of our cargo."

To this I replied, "Captain 'Henry,' act without reference to me—do what you think your duty. For my part, sir, I concur with you: burn her by all means—I am not afraid. I have made up my mind, and am indifferent to my fate, if only the Federals do not get the vessel."

To this Captain "Henry" made no reply, but turned abruptly away and walked aft, where his officers were standing in a group. With them he held a hurried consultation, and then, coming to where I was seated, exclaimed—

"It is too late to burn her now. The Yankee is almost on board of us. We must surrender!"

During all this time the enemy's fire never ceased. Round shot and shell were ploughing up the water about us. They flew before, behind, and above—everywhere but into us; and, although I knew that the first of those heavy missiles which should strike must be fatal to many, perhaps to all, yet so angry did I feel that I could have forfeited my own life if, by so doing, I could have baulked the Federals of their prey.

At this moment we were not more than half a mile from our tormentor; for we had luffed up in the wind, and stopped our engine. Suddenly, with a deep humming sound, came a hundred-pound bolt. This shot was fired from their long gun amidships, and passed just over my head, between myself and the captain, who was standing on the bridge a little above me.

"By Jove! don't they intend to give us

quarter, or show us some mercy at any rate?" cried Captain "Henry." "I have surrendered."

And now from the Yankee came a stentorian hail. "Steamer ahoy! haul down that flag, or we will pour a broadside into you!"

Captain "Henry" then ordered the man at the wheel to lower the colours; but he replied, with true British pluck, that "he had sailed many times under that flag, but had never yet seen it hauled down; and," added he, "I cannot do it now." We were sailing under British colours, and the man at the helm was an Englishman.

All this time repeated hails of "Haul down that flag, or we will sink you!" greeted us, until, at last, some one, I know not who, seeing how hopeless it must be to brave them longer, took it upon himself to execute Captain "Henry's" order, and lowered the English ensign.

CHAPTER IV.

WE are boarded by an Officer from the Yankee—The U.S. Steamer *Connecticut*— An Officer, but no Gentleman—Strange state of Yankee discipline—Scenes on board of the *Greyhound* after her capture—" Ain't ye skeared ?"—A proud boast.

BEFORE the acknowledgment of our surrender had been made, a keg containing some twenty or thirty thousand dollars, equivalent in value to about six thousand pounds sterling, had been brought up on deck and consigned to the deep; whilst all my despatches and letters of introduction, of which latter I had many, were consumed in the furnaces very shortly afterwards.

We were boarded by a boat's crew from our captor, under the command of the executive officer, Mr. Kempf. Mounting the side, he walked up to Captain "Henry" and said—

"Good day to you, Captain; I am glad to see you. This is a very fine vessel, and a valuable one. Will you be good enough to let me see your papers?"

To this Captain "Henry" replied, "Good day to yourself, sir; but as to my being happy to see you, I cannot really say that I am. I have no papers."

The Federal lieutenant then said, "Well, Captain, your presence is required on board the United States steamer *Connecticut*, Captain Almy commanding; and, if you can prove yourself all right, you will, no doubt, be permitted to go."

To this Captain "Henry" made no response, but, stepping into the cabin, donned his coat, and, returning on deck, said, "Now, sir, I am ready; shall we go?" Without further parley the two stepped together into the boat which was lying alongside, and immediately pulled for the *Connecticut*.

One Mr. Swasey was left in charge of our luckless *Greyhound*—an officer as unfit for authority as any who has ever trodden the deck of a man-of-war. His subordinates were, I imagine, well acquainted with his character and abilities; at all events, they treated his orders not with respect, but ridicule.

"Now, sergeant," said he, addressing the sergeant of marines, "look out for your men, and I will look out for mine. By the way, though, station one man here to guard the spirit-room, and don't let any one go below; the first man I catch doing so I will blow his brains out, I will; I would not let my own father have a drink."

He might possibly have resisted the solicitations of a thirsty parent, but he proved quite unable to withstand those of the men. He had hardly finished speaking when a seaman, whom, by his *illigant* brogue, I recognised at once for a true son of Erin, approached and addressed Mr. Swasey with all the native eloquence and pathos of his country—

"Ah, Mr. Swasey, will yees be afther lettin' me have a small bottle of whiskey to kape out the could?"

The colloquy that ensued was ludicrous in the extreme, terminating in a victory of the Irish sailor over the Federal officer.

This example of successful insubordination once set was soon followed; and in every instance Mr. Swasey yielded to the remonstrances, or rather to the mutinous appeals, of his men.

"Here," suddenly exclaimed he, catching a glimpse of myself, "sergeant of the guard! serjeant of the guard! put a man in front of this door, and give him orders to stab this woman if she dares to attempt to come out."

This order, so highly becoming an officer and a gentleman, so courteous in its language, and withal so necessary to the safety and preservation of the prize, was given in a menacing voice and in the very words I have used. I record them for the purpose of showing how admirably the Federal Government has selected its naval officers, and how punctually and gallantly they fulfilled the instructions of their superiors. *Parcere subjectis* must have been blotted out from the edition of the ancient poet read in those schools which had the honour of educating them.

Mr. Swasey then came to the cabin door and introduced himself in these brief but delicate words : " Now, ain't ye skeared ?"

My blood was roused, and I replied, " No, I am not; I was never frightened at a Yankee in my life!"

This retort of mine seemed to surprise him, as he walked away without another word. The effects of his displeasure, however, soon made themselves felt. To my ineffable disgust, the officers, and even the men, were permitted to walk at pleasure into my cabin, which I had hoped would have been respected as the sanctuary of a modest girl. In this hope, as in so many others, I calculated far too much upon the forbearance and humanity of Yankees; and these qualities were seldom exhibited when their enemies were defenceless and, consequently, at their mercy.

Officers and men now proceeded to help themselves to the private wines of the captain, in spite of the protest of the sentry who had been placed in front of my door, and of whom it is but justice to say that nature had qualified him to command when his superiors would have done well to obey.

While these scenes were being enacted, my maid, and a coloured woman whom Captain "Henry" was conveying to a lady in Bermuda, were subjected to the rude familiarities of the prize crew.

At this moment one of the *Connecticut's* officers, a Mr. Reveille, walked up to me and said, "Do you know that it was I who fired the shot that passed close over your head?"

"Was it?" replied I. "Should you like to know what I said of the gunner?"

"I should like to know."

"That man, whoever he may be, is an arrant coward to fire upon a defenceless ship after her surrender."

To this rejoinder of mine, more sincere perhaps than prudent, he made no reply, but left the cabin with an embarrassed laugh.

CHAPTER V.

An eventful Meeting—A Gentleman at last—A Wife's Apology—Mr. Hardinge—I am disappointed—A pleasant Exchange—Farewell to Mr. Swasey—A ludicrous Incident—Captain Henry's best Boots—I am discovered through treachery.

SCARCELY had the discomfited Yankee betaken himself, to my intense satisfaction, upon deck, when I noticed a young officer who had just come over the side.

He crossed the deck by the wheel and approached the cabin. I saw at a glance he was made of other stuff than his comrades who had preceded him; and I confess my attention was riveted by the presence of a gentleman—the first, I think my readers will allow, whom I had met in the hour of my distress.

A woman and a wife may, perhaps, be forgiven if, in a work which treats of more serious adventures than those of love, she indulges in a very brief reminiscence of the impression produced upon her by her future husband. Critics may smile; but I flatter myself that Englishwomen, so widely and so justly famed for conjugal devotion, will forgive me.

His dark brown hair hung down on his shoulders; his eyes were large and bright. Those who judge of beauty by regularity of feature only could not have pronounced him strictly handsome. Neither Phidias nor Praxiteles would have chosen the subject for a model of Grecian grace; but the fascination of his manner was such, his every movement was so much that of a refined gentleman, that my Southern "proclivities," strong as they were, yielded for a moment to the impulses of my heart, and I said to myself, "Oh, what a good fellow that must be!"

To my secret disappointment, he passed by the cabin without entering or making any inquiries about me. I asked one of the *Connecticut's* officers who was close to me the name of the new arrival in this party of pleasure. "Lieutenant Hardinge," was his reply.

Soon afterwards I heard the following conversation, which I perfectly well remember, and which I transcribe *verbatim*, between Mr. Swasey and Mr. Hardinge :—

Mr. Swasey.—" Hallo, Hardinge, anything up? what is it?"

Mr. Hardinge.—" Yes, sir; by order of Captain Almy, I have come to relieve you of the command of this vessel. It is his order that you proceed forthwith on board the *Connecticut:* you will be pleased to hand over to me the papers you have in relation to this vessel."

Mr. Swasey.—" It is a lie! it is a lie! it ain't no such thing! I won't believe it. You have been lately juggling with the captain. Confound it! that is the way you always do!"

Mr. Hardinge.—" Mr. Swasey, I am but obeying my orders; you must not insult me. If you continue to do so, I shall report you."

Mr. Swasey cooled at once, I suppose, as I heard nothing further on his side. He promptly handed over his orders, as desired by Mr. Hardinge, jumped into the boat alongside, and I caught the last sound of his charming voice as he uttered the word of command, "Give way there!" to the boat's crew.

He returned to the *Connecticut,* and so passes out of this story. If its pages ever meet his eye, perhaps they may make him reflect that courtesy to a lady is compatible with the sternest duties of an officer, and that forbearance to the vanquished has always been the attribute of a truly brave man.

Within a few minutes of the departure of our sometime prizemaster, Mr. Hardinge, now in command, issued his orders to the sergeant of marines as to how the men were to be posted; and I overheard, not without an emotion of pleasure, the sergeant telling one of our officers that, although Mr. Hardinge might be a strict disciplinarian on duty, there was not a finer young fellow in the navy, and that his men would follow him anywhere.

Before long Mr. Hardinge came aft, and, bowing to me, asked permission to enter my cabin for a moment.

"Certainly," I replied; "I know that I am a prisoner."

"I am now in command of this vessel," said he; "and I beg you will consider yourself a passenger, not a prisoner."

With the commencement of Mr. Hardinge's command—I may safely say, from the very moment he came on board—the conduct of the prize crew underwent a complete change; and one of the Yankee officers remarked, in my hearing, that, although Hardinge was young, he knew how to command other men, and had learnt early in life the secret and the value of discipline.

Half an hour, or thereabouts, elapsed, and I was reconciling myself to my captivity, when the return on board of Captain "Henry" was the occasion of a ludicrous incident which amused me more than perhaps my readers will suppose. I despair of describing it as it appeared to me: perhaps the reaction of my own feelings (such as we experience after passing safely through sudden and serious danger) gave it a zest beyond its real flavour.

It was on this wise. Captain "Henry," coming on board, caught sight of a Federal sailor strutting about on the cotton bales in a pair of his (Captain "Henry's") very best boots—boots which the captain most particularly cherished.

"Here, you fellow, what are you doing with my boots? Take them off at once, or I shall report you to the officer in command for stealing."

"But, sir," said the sailor, loath to part with his contraband goods, "I bought them from a messmate of mine, and chucked my own into the sea."

This subterfuge, however, did not impose upon Mr. Hardinge's sense of honour and discipline. The ancient mariner had to remove the stolen boots and return barefooted to his ship.

The officers and crew of the *Greyhound*, together with my fellow-passengers Mr. Pollard and Mr. Newell, were taken on board the *Connecticut*. The captain, steward, cook, and cabin-boy, myself and my maid, remained prisoners on board the prize.

Before we were taken—indeed, when we sailed from Wilmington—it had been agreed that " Belle Boyd " should be for the time ignored, and that " Mrs. Lewis " should take her place. It was obvious that, in the event of capture, I should run less risk, suffer fewer privations, and be exposed to less indignity under an assumed name. Conceive, then, my surprise and indignation when I found that my secret had been revealed through the treachery of an unworthy countryman.

Captain " Henry " told me that the *Minnie*, a blockade-runner like the *Greyhound*, which had been captured the day before by the *Connecticut*, had been the means of our own mishap. There can be no doubt that one of her officers was a traitor to the cause of his country, and had, through fear, or actuated by some other unworthy motive, sacrificed those he should have defended with his life.

It is with reluctance that I record this instance of dishonour on the part of a Southerner; but I am resolved to be an impartial historian, and, although often severe to the Yankees, by dint of telling plainly their shortcomings, I will not shrink from the truth when it is unfavourable to my countrymen.

CHAPTER VI.

Bound North—We are taken in tow—Our first Evening at Sea—We arrive at Fortress Monroe—Commodore Guerte Gansevoorte comes on board in James River—We are paroled by him—His Indignation against Mr. Hardinge for flying the English Ensign—The Commodore's conduct whilst on board—Arrival at New York—We go on Shore—I visit Niblos' Theatre—Return aboard and departure for Boston—Love triumphant!

Boats were continually passing to and fro between the "Prize," as she was designated, and the *Connecticut*, with orders and counter-orders, until the proximity of the vessels grew wearisome. I was relieved to hear that we were about to start, and my pleasure did not diminish when, at 8 p.m., the command was given to get under steam and proceed northward, keeping just astern of the *Connecticut*, which would accompany us. Heart-sick at the turn that the tide of fortune had taken, I retired to my couch and endeavoured to sleep. But prison walls could not be banished from my imagination, and the attempt was vain.

The next morning, at daylight, I was aroused by loud hailing from the Yankee cruiser as she passed close to us, ordering that we should " heave to " whilst she sent a boat on board. We presently learned that our destination was to be Fortress Monroe, and that we were to be towed thither behind the *Connecticut*. Hawsers were passed to us by means of boats, and, when these tow-lines had been well secured, both vessels steamed ahead.

It was the second evening after our surrender that Captain "Henry," Mr. Hardinge, and myself were seated together close by the wheel. The moon shone beautifully clear, lighting up everything with a brightness truly magnificent; the ocean, just agitated by a slight breeze that swept over its surface, looked like one vast bed of sparkling diamonds, and the rippling of the little waves, as they struck the vessel's side, seemed but the soft accompaniment to the vocal music with which Captain "Henry" had been regaling us.

> "Here will we sit, and let the sounds of music
> Creep in our ears: soft stillness, and the night,
> Become the touches of sweet harmony."

Presently Captain "Henry" went forward

on the bridge and conversed with Mr. Hall, the officer on watch. We two were left to ourselves; and Mr. Hardinge quoted some beautiful passages from Byron and Shakspeare. Then, in a decidedly Claude Melnotte style, he endeavoured to paint the " home to which, if love could but fulfil its prayers, this heart would lead thee!" And from poetry he passed on to plead an oft-told tale. . . . .

Situated as I was, and having known him for so short a time, a very practical thought flitted through my brain. If he felt all that he professed to feel for me, he might in future be useful to us; so, when he asked me " to be his wife," I told him that " his question involved serious consequences," and that " he must not expect an answer until I should arrive at Boston."

During our voyage Mr. Hardinge was so

kind and courteous that Captain "Henry" took a great fancy to him, and swore eternal friendship to one of whom he afterwards spoke as "the most thorough gentleman from Yankee-land that he had ever met with."

The morning which succeeded the romantic episode slightly sketched above beheld the *Connecticut* and *Greyhound* lying to off the Capes. A fog detained us in uncertainty as to our whereabouts for some time; and, when it lifted, we steamed up Hampton Roads.

I sat on the little deck aft, watching with interest all that I saw, and listened alternately to the captain and Mr. Hardinge as they conversed on various topics. From the latter I ascertained that "Beast Butler" was in command at Fortress Monroe, and from him I could expect but little courtesy.

As we neared our anchorage, I made out distinctly the grim outline of the fortress, rising in its majesty and strength. I compared myself to the fly nearing the cunning old spider, who was eagerly watching for the moment when it should become entangled in his intricate web.

My capture had been telegraphed to those in authority. The *Connecticut* had cast off from us about half-way up the river, and had gone onward to the mouth of the James, where Admiral Lee then was; but the *Greyhound*, when opposite the pier of the Baltimore steamers, came to an anchor. Mr. Hardinge went on board the flag-ship *Minnesota* to report. He was absent about two hours, and when he returned we got under way, proceeding up stream to join the *Connecticut*. Mr. Hardinge could tell me nothing of my probable destination, and I suspected that I was to be incarcerated in Fortress Monroe — there to remain I knew not how long, perhaps for ever!

After about three-quarters of an hour we again anchored, this time close by the iron-clad *Roanoke*, Commodore Guerte Gansevoorte, who was acting in the place of Admiral Lee.

The Admiral was then up the James River, ostensibly for the purpose of fighting the "rebels." But, much to the disgust of his officers and of the Federal naval department (if we may believe the journals of the day), he merely re-enacted the farce of sinking vessels and driving in spikes across the river from bank to bank, to prevent the "cowardly rebels" from doing what he dared not—giving battle.

Just after we brought up it blew a perfect

hurricane, followed by a drenching rain, which lasted for some time. Such weather was, in itself, sufficiently dreary and discouraging; nor did the sensation that we were dragging toward a lee-shore of uninviting appearance greatly comfort me. I felt, indeed, some pleasure when I thought that the Federals would, perhaps, lose their prize—a feeling which Captain "Henry" fully shared. In this cheerful desire we were disappointed; for, as the captain afterwards remarked, "the vessel was admirably handled by Mr. Hardinge."

Amid whistling wind and pouring rain an English ensign had been flying from the stern, and the Federal flag, which had been hoisted when coming up the bay, was conspicuous at the fore. This seems to have excited the ire of the Commodore, who, when the storm had passed, boarded us, with solemn displeasure written upon his face.

I am positive that I should have had a better opinion of the man had he remained in his own vessel; for I now saw him far from sober. One of the officers remarked that "it was after four o'clock," by way of an apology to the "youngling," as he was pleased to term Mr. Hardinge.

Commodore Guerte Gansevoorte was not over-polite, and, upon reaching the deck, swore roundly and lustily, d——ing right and left, and was evidently—

> "As *wild* a mannered man
> As ever scuttled ship or cut a throat."

But then, as it was a wet day, he had evidently been taking something hot within to guard him from the cold.

When the Commodore approached my

cabin door, I heard Mr. Hardinge say, "Sir, a lady is dressing there. Will you be kind enough to wait? She is my passenger, and I am responsible for her." I had finished, however; and the coloured servant, opening the door, said to Mr. Hardinge, "De lady am ready, massa." On this the Commodore remarked, "Ugh! got to that has it?"

His *entrée* into the cabin was truly imposing; for, stumbling over piled-up cotton, he staggered, then slipped, and made his descent and bow at the same moment. His aide, Mr. —— (executive officer, I believe), looked mortified, and seemed somewhat ashamed whilst following in the great man's rear with less of the former's peculiar dignity.

"So," said the Commodore, "this is Miss Belle Boyd, is it?" Just then Captain

"Henry" came in, and, turning round, he exclaimed, "What! by ——! George, old fel——;" then, remembering his official position, stopped suddenly in the midst of the exclamation. I do not remember much of the conversation which ensued, but noticed that the executive officer was sober and apparently disgusted with the conduct of his superior.

The Commodore at first would not be seated, but did so after a few moments' further conversation. Champagne and glasses were brought in; and he soon became exceedingly communicative, and, with an oath, swore that Captain "Henry" should have a parole extending as far as Boston. Asking for pen, ink, and paper, which I immediately procured, he bade the executive officer write the required parole, and signed it with his own hand. Mr.

Hardinge asked for the document, or, at least, a copy of the same; but he would not comply, declaring that "his orders were sufficient."

As he rose to depart, he turned to me and said, in answer to a request of mine, "You, miss, when you arrive at New York, can go on shore, provided Mr. Hardinge accompanies you. And," he added, attempting some compliments, "I will not enforce a written parole with you, but will take a verbal promise. Don't be at all alarmed—you shan't go to prison." The Commodore then left us. His descent into the boat was executed in the same dignified and gentlemanly manner as had been his *entrée* into my presence; and I felt very thankful when Mr. Hall informed me that the great man had gone.

Half an hour may have passed, when a boat came from the *Roanoke* to inform Mr. Hardinge that the Commodore had ordered that the *Greyhound* should be brought under the lee of the iron-clad. My heart sank, for it seemed that, after all, he had been playing with us; still more so when, as we rounded to under the *Roanoke's* stern, I heard the Commodore threatening through his trumpet to blow us out of the water. In his condition he might have done anything; so our anxiety may well be imagined.

Reverting for a moment to the English ensign before mentioned as flying aboard the *Greyhound*, I may describe how the Commodore, when he saw it, shouted furiously, "Haul down that —— rag!" Mr. Hardinge ventured to suggest that this was a violation of the law regarding neutral vessels captured in time of war. To which the Commodore made answer by saying, "I don't want any —— sea-lawyer's arguments!" and he afterwards sent a written order to Mr. Hardinge, forbidding him to fly the English flag.

As we lay beside the *Roanoke*, vague threats were made and contradictory orders given. Now we were told to be "off at once," then "not to think of moving at present;" until Mr. Hardinge grew restless at such constant supervision, and, taking advantage of a command to quit the station, steamed away, without waiting for anything more. Right glad were we when the shades of night hid from our view the monster iron-clad, and yet, thankful to Captain Almy, of the *Connecticut*, who, *not* being drunk, stopped us somewhat farther down, delaying our departure for the very sensible reason that a gale of wind was blowing.

Early the next day a steam-tug from the fortress went alongside of the *Connecticut*, and the officers, passengers, and men of the *Minnie* and *Greyhound* were transferred to her, with the exception of Mr. Pollard, who was sent aboard of us to proceed to Boston. When the tug steamed by, handkerchiefs and caps were waved; and I was afterwards informed that they would have cheered me had they been permitted to do so. Fresh meat, vegetables, and ice (the latter of which we esteemed a luxury, as the weather was very warm) had been procured on shore for our consumption.

At length we proceeded to sea, bound for Boston, Massachusetts, *viâ* New York, where it was intended that we should touch for coal. I will pass over this portion of the voyage, merely remarking that it was as pleasant as could be expected under the circumstances, and that the officers did all in their power to make things comfortable for us.

As we neared New York thick fog completely enshrouded the coast, but our speed was not slackened. We pressed forward, often passing vessels so near as hardly to give them breathing room. Part of one night we lay off Barnegat; for the fog had become so thick that the pilot did not judge it safe for us to proceed. But when morning broke a brisk wind sprang up, enabling us to see the outline of Sandy Hook. As we passed on up the harbour the motion became less disagreeable to me, and, a comfortable seat having been placed on the deck-house, I enjoyed a panorama of sea and shore scarce equalled in beauty by the approach to any other city in the world.

Off Quarantine we were boarded by the health officer, who, after asking several questions, permitted us to go on our way; and we came to an anchor off Navy Yard. Mr. Hardinge went on shore to report his arrival, while Mr. Hall proceeded to bring the vessel alongside the coal-hulk. When Mr. Hardinge returned in the afternoon the dock was filled with gazers, who, excited by that morbid curiosity exhibited by the world in general, had come to witness, as they supposed, my debarkation. In this they were somewhat disappointed, for everything had been arranged so nicely that not one of the many there assembled knew when I went on shore. A Navy

Yard tug dropped alongside the *Greyhound*, and, with the assistance of Captain H., I was soon snugly settled in the tug's wheelhouse.

Captain "Henry" and Mr. Hardinge accompanied me. We crossed to the New York side of the river, and landed at the foot of Canal Street. Procuring a carriage, we drove to a friend's house, where I took from off my person the money which I had concealed about me, and the weight of which at times had almost made me faint. This money belonged to myself and Captain "Henry," and was not, as Yankee papers averred, part of the ship's money we had thrown overboard previous to our capture. Captain "Henry" placed our money in the bank, where it was safe from further molestation.

We visited Niblo's Theatre to witness

the performance of "Bel Demonio." What a contrast did the gay, wealthy city of New York afford at this period to my own sorrow-stricken land! Here there was no sign of want or poverty. No woe-begone faces could I see in that assemblage: all was life and animation. Though war raged within a short distance, its horrors had little influence on the butterflies of the empire city; whilst, in my own dear native country, all was sad and heart-rending. We were sacrificing lives upon the altar of Liberty; while the North sacrificed hers upon the altar of Mammon.

Next morning Mr. Hardinge called for me, and, after having finished my shopping, we returned to the *Greyhound*, which now lay in mid-stream. Captain "Henry" had gone on board before us, as also had Mr. Pollard. I forgot to mention that this gentleman had been paroled by Mr. Hardinge for the night.

For the rest of the time, above four hours, that we remained at New York we were besieged by visitors—old acquaintances, who were allowed to see me. Amongst them were several naval and military officers. About 4 p.m. the pilot came on board, and, bidding adieu to the capital of " Shoddy," away we steamed for Boston.

The weather was lovely, the water smooth as glass, and the sky cloudless as that of Italy. On each side of us, along the shores of the Sound, were beautiful residences, whose owners, as they strolled over their lawns, or sat smoking on terrace or balcony, appeared to think little, and care less, about the war. We glided past many craft, which lay with white sails that flapped against their masts. I was melancholy; I hardly knew why. The face of nature wore its very sweetest smile; everything was propitious; yet I was not pleased, and sought the cabin.

Mr. Hardinge, in a few moments, followed me, and then he repeated a declaration on which I need not expatiate, as it concerned ourselves more than any one else. So generous and noble was he in everything that I could not but acknowledge that my heart was his. I firmly believe that God intended us to meet and love; and, to make the story short, I told him that "I would be his wife." Although our politics differed, "women," thought I, "can sometimes work wonders; and may not he, who is of Northern birth, come by degrees to love, for my sake, the ill-used South?"

Then Captain "Henry" came into the cabin; and, when we told him all, he joined our hands together, saying—

"Hardinge, you are a good fellow, and I love you, boy! Miss Belle deserves a good husband; and I know no one more worthy of her than yourself. May you both be happy!"

CHAPTER VII.

Arrival in Boston—Our plan for re-capturing the *Greyhound* frustrated—Captain "Henry's" Escape—How it was managed—Marshal Keyes comes on Board—The Search for the Captain—A false Report of his Arrest—I communicate with him—He leaves for New York—I bid adieu to the *Greyhound*—My Quarters on Shore—I am paroled for the City—Newspaper Rumours—Mr. Hardinge proceeds to Washington in my behalf—My Mother telegraphs to the Marshal—She is not permitted to see me—Politeness of the British Consul—I write a Letter to the Secretary of the Navy—Am pronounced insane—I am liberated—Mr. Hardinge and his Officers are placed under Arrest—Mr. Pollard is sent to Fort Warren—I leave for Canada.

WHEN we neared Boston I saw the grim

walls of Fort Warren; and a shudder passed over me as I inwardly wondered if that would be my home. All my bright dreams of "merrie England," of "bonnie Scotland," and of a tour on the Continent, were, for the time, banished. The future lowered dark and uncertain. Had not some good spirit whispered hope, I should scarcely have borne up against these gloomy impressions. But I was still "Mrs. Lewis," and might yet escape :—

> "For, lo! the heavier Grief weighed down,
>   The higher Hope was raised."

When we were first captured it had been agreed that, on our voyage north, an attempt should be made to retake the *Greyhound*.

The project, however, had been abandoned, not from any lack of zeal, but from force of circumstances; for Captain Almy had refused to put on board of us our chief engineer and first officer, without whom the attempt could not possibly succeed.

Another plan, quietly prepared by us previously, and which had reference to the escape of Captain "Henry," had better luck. Whilst we were coming to an anchor off the Boston Navy Yard, and Mr. Hardinge was forward, giving orders to the men, Captain "Henry," Mr. Pollard, and myself were aft, seated in the cabin. I asked the two Yankee pilots if they would join us and partake of a glass of wine. To this they of course assented, and drank freely; for doubtless such wine but seldom passed their lips. I then nodded to Captain "Henry," who, carelessly putting on his hat, and taking his umbrella in his hand, walked up on deck and went aft, where he stood for some moments. Everything seemed to favour us, for Mr. Hardinge had called a harbour-boat alongside, that he might go ashore to report his arrival.

Before starting, Mr. Hardinge came to me and asked "where his papers were;" when I replied that I thought they must be "in the lower cabin, where he had been dressing himself." He immediately went down to fetch them; and this was the golden opportunity for which we had waited. In less time than it takes me to write it, Captain "Henry" stepped into the boat, which dropped slowly astern with the tide; and, when Mr. Hardinge reappeared, the captain was safe on land.

The whole scene was amusing in the extreme to those who understood it, so well had it been managed. When Mr. Hardinge found his boat gone, he came to the conclusion that the waterman had grown tired of waiting and had pulled off; so, calling another, he stepped into it and proceeded to report his prize.

In about three hours he returned, bringing with him the United States Marshal, Keyes, and several other gentlemen of position and influence in Boston, whom he introduced to me.

The Marshal then asked for Captain "Henry."

"I think he is on deck," I replied.

Mr. Hardinge went to find him, leaving the other gentlemen to converse with Mr. Pollard and myself. From me, however, they did not learn much, for I sustained the supposititious character of "Mrs. Lewis" with becoming gravity; and it was not until several days after that they became quite sure that I was none other than the celebrated "Belle Boyd."

In a few moments Marshal Keyes, followed by Mr. Hardinge, entered the cabin, the Marshal exclaiming, "Captain 'Henry' has escaped!"

"What!" said I; "it is impossible! only a few moments ago he was here!" and I looked very serious, though all the while I was laughing in my sleeve, saying to myself, "Again I have got the better of the Yankees!" The vessel was thoroughly searched—nay, I believe that it was fumigated, or "smoked," to get the captain out; for Marshal Keyes was "positive" that he was on board—so he informed me on his way to the hotel.

Captain "Henry's" escape caused much sensation. Detectives, great and small, were thrown into a flutter of excitement, and the Boston police, whom Marshal Keyes affirmed to be the "best in the world," were all astir that the fugitive might be lodged in Fort Warren. These myrmidons of Northern power were, certainly, not favoured with a very accurate description of Captain "Henry." Some declared that he wore a black hat, others that he had a white covering to his head; some that his nose was aquiline, others that it was decidedly *retroussé*. Such contradictions bewildered the police, whose efforts resulted in a wild-goose chase.

Late on the evening of the escape Marshal Keyes was jubilant over a supposed capture at Portland, Maine, whither he had telegraphed to have any suspicious character arrested. The Portland captive proved to be not the gentleman of whom they were in quest, but a harmless English tourist, who was, no doubt, much aggrieved at his unlawful detention.

When the Marshal informed me of the captain's arrest at Portland, I knew that there must be some mistake, and could hardly restrain my laughter; for all this time Captain "Henry" was lying *perdue* in Boston, under an assumed name. I was well aware of the captain's residence, and through the medium of a friend received several communications from him. In my replies I assured him that he was already as good as free. For two days he stayed quietly at the hotel, and then I heard that he had set off for Canada, *via* New York.

Detectives had been sent all over the country to intercept him; but it was one of the best managed escapes from the toils of the " 'cute" Yankees that ever took place. Captain "Henry" actually remained for some time at one of the largest hotels in Broadway, where he saw many of his old friends, who, fortunately, did not recognise him.

Many and various were the reports of this affair that found circulation; but, singularly enough, it was the United States officers on board the *Greyhound*, and not "Mrs. Lewis," who had to bear the brunt of suspicion, though I was really the one to blame. I was delighted at being a *non-suspect*, by way of a change, and could thoroughly appreciate the chagrin of Marshal Keyes. He had prophesied that this was a case of capture with which Lord Lyons, at Washington, would not dare to interfere, as Captain "Henry"—to use the Marshal's own words—"was an officer of the

Confederate navy, and therefore not an Englishman." To this view of international law I politely assented, thinking that, if Captain "Henry" could only reach a place of safety, it would matter very little how the Marshal classified him.

The *Greyhound* was hauled alongside a wharf, and an immense concourse of people assembled to witness my coming ashore; for it had been telegraphed from New York, and then again from the station in Boston Bay, that "Belle Boyd" was aboard the prize. Marshal Keyes was most courteous, and stated that he had procured a suite of rooms for me at the Tremont House, where I was to remain until my fate was definitely settled. This, he added, would be in a very few days; when he should either have the "supreme pleasure" of taking me to Canada, or the "unpleasant task" of delivering me over to the tender mercies of the commandant of Fort Warren.

The public journals were indefatigable in noticing all my movements. The Sunday-morning papers informed their readers that "Miss Belle Boyd would attend Divine service at the Old —— Church during the forenoon." The week-day news-sheets gave notice that "Miss Belle Boyd, in company with her gallant captor, whose sympathies, no doubt, were with the South, were seen out driving the day before;" and, as a climax, the bulletin boards announced that "Belle Boyd had been sent to the Fitchburg Gaol!" Such were a few of the many *canards* that flew abroad during my stay in the "modern Athens."

I had been there about ten days, when Mr. Hardinge, fearing that the "Fitchburg

Gaol" story might be but the shadow of a coming event, proceeded to Washington, to procure, if possible, my release. Having letters of introduction to many of the leading and influential men there, he induced them to use their power in my behalf.

Although I was but thirty-six hours' railway-journey from my mother, who had telegraphed to the Marshal to allow her to come and see me, she was not permitted to do so; and none of her letters reached me, they being probably intercepted. But, if letters of affection were thus stopped, there were, happily, other channels than the postal department by which friendly comfort could arrive. Many Boston ladies and gentlemen visited me, despite the Government spies who hovered about my quarters.

After being kept in suspense for three weeks, I forwarded, through Marshal Keyes, a letter to Gideon Welles, Secretary of the Navy at Washington, telling him that " I really was Belle Boyd, and wished to go to Canada that I might communicate with my mother."

The Marshal received a telegram in answer, saying that " Miss Boyd and her servants should be escorted beyond the lines into Canada, and that, *if I was again caught in the United States, or by the United States authorities, I should be shot.*" This was on a Sunday evening; and the Marshal advised me to depart with all convenient speed, as I had only twenty-four hours' grace. I promised to start on Monday, at 5 p.m. It was impossible to go sooner, no trains running through to Montreal on Sunday.

The "Washington Republican" got possession of my letter to Gideon Welles, and published it *in extenso*, with the remark that I was "insane," and had been, on that account, released by the Government. For this verdict of lunacy I thank them, if it contributed in any degree to mitigate my sentence. There certainly existed sufficient method in my madness to make me appreciate the advantage of having the promised shooting deferred until they caught me again; and I felt much obliged to members of Congress and others who used their influence in my behalf.

Mr. Hardinge was sent for early on Monday morning by Admiral Stringham, but he assured me that he would soon return. The day passed by, however, without any sign of him, and I began to wonder what had happened, when I received the following letter, in his handwriting:—

" My dear Miss Belle,

"It is all up with me. Mr. Hall, the engineers, and myself are prisoners, charged with complicity in the escape of Captain H——. The Admiral says that it looks bad for us; so I have adopted a very good motto, viz., 'Face the music!' and, come what may, the officers under me shall be cleared. I have asked permission of the Admiral to come and bid you good-bye. I hope that his answer will be in the affirmative."

This was written on board the receiving ship *Ohio*. Its receipt made me feel very unhappy, for I feared that circumstantial evidence was against Mr. Hardinge, and that, ere long, he would, although perfectly innocent, share with poor Mr. Pollard a casemate in Fort Warren. But suddenly the object of my thoughts made his appearance. He informed me that the Admiral had allowed him and his officers to be paroled until sundown, and that he had availed himself of this privilege to come instantly to me.

Mr. Pollard, my fellow-passenger from Wilmington, against whom the Yankee journals were exceedingly vituperative, had on the Sunday morning been conveyed to Fort Warren, and there immured for the crime of being distasteful to those in authority. Suffice it to say of Mr. Pollard's subsequent adventures that he was paroled to the city of Brooklyn, owing to his very bad health; since which I have not heard of him.

The time for my departure from Boston came at last. The Tremont Hotel was left, and the railway dépôt was reached. Marshal Keyes endeavoured to make himself agreeable, and was very busy in getting my baggage checked and my ticket taken before the train moved away. The Marshal, I may add, was my courteous companion to the boundary-line between Canada and the United States. With a sad heart I had bidden good-bye to Mr. Hardinge, although I trusted that he would soon rejoin me; and I enjoyed the delightful prospect of breathing free Canadian air.

Yes, I should be free! Free from prison bars and irksome confinement; but, alas! an exile! Each step towards freedom carried me farther and farther from my native land; whilst, did I turn back, a heavy penalty awaited me. My father dead, and my dear mother far away! Truly I was alone in the wide, wide world! And I had left one generous heart behind that I knew would miss me sorely.

CHAPTER VIII.

Arrival at Montreal—Niagara—A System of Espionage still around me—I depart for Europe—Passage across the Atlantic—Arrival in London—I meet Mr. Hardinge once more—Our Marriage—Comments of the Press.

Upon arriving at Montreal, I proceeded to the "St. Lawrence Hall." Captain "Henry" and his wife had proposed that I should join them at Niagara; but, not having heard from them for some time, I waited till I could ascertain their exact whereabouts. In Montreal I met many

Southern families, refugees, and many Confederate sympathizers. The British provinces were at this time a haven of rest for American exiles—much as England has always been to the victims of persecution on the European continent. I learnt that my friends at Niagara were expecting me, and accordingly set off to join them, the Guards serenading me just before my departure.

Niagara, with its sublime scenery, I will not attempt to describe. We were stopping at the Clifton House, and from my windows I could plainly see the Yankee side of the Falls. There, lower down, was the Suspension Bridge, offering almost irresistible temptation to cross from Canada to the States. We heard, on good authority, that above a hundred thousand dollars was being expended on the retaking of Captain "Henry" and myself. Spies were stationed on the bridge to watch and, if possible, to entrap us, should we by chance be foolish enough to venture within their power.

About a week after our arrival at Niagara we noticed, at the *table d'hôte*, two very foppishly-dressed men, with thin, waxed mustaches *à la Napoléon,* and who apparently took great seeming interest in the movements of our entire party. We watched them closely, and were very soon convinced beyond doubt that they were Yankee detectives. Shortly after this discovery we left for Quebec. It was in the morning, about eight o'clock, that we quitted Niagara and proceeded by rail to Toronto, where we arrived about noon. Imagine our surprise at finding the fair imitation dandies, whom we had left quietly at the Clifton House, watching for us at the Toronto terminus. It transpired that they had seen us going, and had quietly entered another car in the same train.

The Canadian journals commented severely upon these fellows, and the system of espionage practised on us whilst we remained in the provinces.

The brace of detectives accompanied us in the steamer that left Toronto a few hours afterwards, and which plies regularly during the summer months between that place and Montreal. We noticed that they hovered round, eyeing us narrowly; and we determined to ascertain whether it was really our party that they were watching. When, therefore, we arrived at our destination, Captain "Henry" repaired to the Donegana

Hotel, whilst I went to the St. Lawrence Hall. In a few hours I learned that one of these fellows had engaged a room at the same hotel where I was stopping; and, when Captain "Henry" called, he told me that the other detective had taken up his abode at the Donegana!

When we resumed our journey to Quebec the spies still dogged us. Captain "Henry" embarked at once for Halifax. I remained some time in Quebec, previous to sailing for Europe; and when, at length, I quitted the American shores, one of the spies endeavoured to secure a passage on board the same vessel! The Canadians, however, detesting his odious calling, insisted that he should be denied this opportunity.

My trip across the Atlantic was, on the whole, favoured by calm weather and a smooth sea; so that I did not suffer much from my enemy the *mal de mer*. Off the banks of Newfoundland we were, to make use of a nautical expression, "tied up" for more than a week by the fogs, amid fields and bergs of ice. The latter I had never before seen; and I gazed upon their majestic grandeur with feelings of awe and amazement. So near, at times, did we pass them, that it is no wonder that I felt somewhat nervous; for, had we struck, it would have been instantaneous death to us all. While crossing the banks we encountered a fearful storm, and for one entire night the steamer rolled and plunged with the force of the waves like some living creature.

> "It was midnight on the ocean,
> And a storm was on the deep!"

But the storm in our case, though violent, did not last long. More moderate weather soon came, and the passengers felt greatly relieved.

When, after entering English waters and passing up channel, and my feet touched the ground once more, I thanked God for our safety. I remember for a long time after, in imagination, I could hear the whir-r-r, whir-r-r of the screw, the creaking of blocks, the flapping of sails, the hoarse, uncouth cries of the sailors, and the clear, distinct voices of the captain and his officers.

Arrived in Liverpool, I remained there for some days at the Washington Hotel, and then proceeded to London. I soon ascertained the address of Mr. Hotze, the Confederate commercial agent, to whom I had had letters of introduction from the

Secretary of State. I reported to the Confederate States Commissioner that the despatches intrusted to me at Wilmington had been destroyed when the *Greyhound* was overhauled, that they might not fall into our enemy's hands.

This report terminated Belle Boyd's connection with the Southern Government for the time being.

> " So from the scene where death and anguish reign,
> And vice and folly drench with blood the plain,
> . . . . I turn!"

Mr. Hotze gave me a letter that had been left with him until I should reach London. Upon opening it, I found that it was from Mr. Hardinge, informing me that he had come to England, but, not being able to learn my whereabouts, had proceeded to Paris, in the faint hope of finding me there. I was deeply touched at this new proof of his honest attachment, and immediately telegraphed a message to him, stating where he would find me in London. Gentle reader, you can, perhaps, imagine for yourself how joyful was our meeting, and in what manner a courtship which had in it much of romance was at length happily terminated.

Our marriage took place on August 25th, 1864, and journalists were pleased to treat the world to some portions of the romance in which we had taken part. The English press was friendly in its tone, but certain Yankee editors became marvellously indignant at the news, and even now they are subject to periodical returns of indignation.

(*Le Moniteur Universel de Paris.*)

"UN MARIAGE A LONDRES.

" On écrit de Londres : Un mariage singulièrement romantique vient d'avoir lieu aujourd'hui, à onze heures, à l'église Saint-James. La fiancée était la célèbre Belle Boyd, l'héroïne de tant d'exploits aventureux pendant la guerre civile d'Amérique et surtout au moment des brillantes campagnes du général Stonewall Jackson, dans la vallée de Shenandoah.

" Mlle Boyd est à peine âgée de vingt ans, d'un caractère très-doux, douée de grands avantages personnels, et liée par la parenté avec quelques-unes des plus influentes familles du Sud. Il paraît que les scènes de la guerre, dont elle était témoin, depuis ces dernières années, avaient développé en elle une énergie et un courage qui se rencontrent rarement chez une femme.

" Les courses à cheval, au milieu de la nuit, à travers marais et forêts, jusque dans les lignes de l'ennemi, d'où elle rapportait aux généraux du Sud des renseignements d'une importance immense, forment le thème de nombreux récits autour des feux de bivouac dans toute l'armée confédérée.

" Elle était tombée entre les mains des fédéraux, mais un jeune officier lui donna les moyens de s'échapper et la suivit dans sa fuite. C'est lui qui, après l'avoir accompagnée en Angleterre, vient de lui donner son nom.

" Dans quelques jours, le jeune époux doit repartir pour les Etats confédérés, où il va s'enrôler comme simple soldat. Ceci a été une des conditions du mariage exigées par la fiancée comme preuve du dévouement de son époux à une cause qu'il combattait dernièrement encore l'épée à la main.

" Le mariage a été célébré sans aucune pompe, mais ensuite un élégant déjeuner préparé à l'hôtel de Brunswick, rue Jermyn, a réuni les jeunes mariés et tous les confédérés de marque et de distinction actuellement à Londres.

" Dans l'après-midi, les deux époux sont partis pour Liverpool, où le futur soldat du Sud va s'embarquer pour les Etats confédérés. On assure que les autorités fédérales ont mis sa tête à prix."

(*Morning Post.*)

"St. James's Church, Piccadilly, was yesterday the scene of a romantic episode in the fratricidal war now raging on the American continent; as, at the altar of that sacred edifice, Miss Belle Boyd, whose name and fame are deservedly cherished in the Southern States, pledged her troth to Mr. Sam Wylde Hardinge, formerly an officer in the Federal naval service. The marriage attracted to the church a considerable number of English and American sympathizers in the cause of the South, anxious to see the lady whose heroism has made her name so famous, and to witness the result of her last captivity, the making captive of the Federal officer under whose guard she was again being conveyed to prison. Miss Boyd, it will be remembered, is the Virginian lady who, during the terrible scenes enacted in the Valley of the Shenandoah, rendered such essential service to General Stonewall Jackson, by procuring for him information of great value as regards the position and condition of the Northern forces, and who signalized her devotion to the cause of her country by so many other services. Capture and imprisonment did not damp her adventurous and patriotic ardour, as she was twice immured, once for seven months, and once for ten months. She was again seized, and, while on board a Federal vessel, on her way to the North, made the acquaintance of Lieutenant Hardinge, with whom, having crossed the Atlantic, she has entered into the bonds of matrimony. Mr. Hardinge needs no excuse for the step he has taken in renouncing his allegiance to the Federal cause and espousing the fair 'rebel,' whom he has now sworn to love, honour, and cherish. Though, in obedience to the wishes of his father, he served for some time in the Federal navy, in which service he rose to be lieutenant, his Southern sympathies were notorious in the North, where it was well known that he had long tendered his resignation, which Mr. Secretary Welles refused to accept; and thus he was forced to continue in a service which he would gladly have renounced long since. Though more than suspected of Southern sympathies, he kept his word when he promised the executive of the Federal navy that the name he bore—a name which had descended to him from a long line of ancestors in Great Britain and America—should not be disgraced, and proved his readiness to perform his duty on many occasions.

"The bride was attended to the altar by Mrs. Edward Robinson Harvey, the bridegroom by Mr. Henry Howard Barber, and the marriage service was read by the Rev. Mr. Paull, of St. James's Chapel, in a manner which deeply impressed all present with the solemn nature of the contract entered into. Amongst the friends of the bride and bridegroom, and of the Confederate cause, who attended were the Hon. General Williams, formerly United States Minister at Constantinople; the Hon. J. O'Sullivan, formerly Minister from Washington at Lisbon; Major Hughes, of the Confederate army; Captain Fearn, Confederate army; the Rev. Frederic Kill Harford (who gave the bride away); Mr. Keen Richards, of Kentucky; Mr. Henry Hotze, Mr. C. Warren Adams, Mrs. Paull, Madame Cerbelle, Mr. Reay, &c.

"At the conclusion of the ceremony the bride and bridegroom and their friends proceeded to the Brunswick Hotel, Jermyn Street, where a choice and well-arranged breakfast was partaken of, and at a fitting moment, towards the conclusion, Mr. Barber, in a most eloquent speech, proposed the health of Mr. and Mrs. Hardinge, eulogizing the services the lady had performed, and prognosticating that the bridegroom would soon win fame in the service on which he is about to enter. The toast, as may be anticipated, was received with much delight, and was replied to by both bride and bridegroom, who expressed their acknowledgments to the many friends they had found in this country. The toast of 'The Queen' was afterwards given by Captain Fearn, who assured the English portion of his hearers that her Majesty was greatly revered in all parts of the Southern States of America—an assertion which was most warmly corroborated by all present, who were qualified to speak from experience. 'President Davis and General Lee,' and many other toasts, followed in due order, till the growing hours warned the bride and bridegroom that it was time to depart for Liverpool. Mr. Hardinge purposes in a few days to leave for the South, whither, in spite of the blockade, he intends to convey a goodly portion of the wedding-cake, for distribution amongst his wife's friends."

The journey referred to above was taken by my husband very shortly after, for the simple purpose of communicating with my family in Virginia. Its results will be shown in the following chapters, in which he will tell his own story.

CHAPTER IX.

Lieutenant Hardinge's Journal—Arrival at Home—A Surprise—A silent Breakfast—Visit to Martinsburg—A pleasant little Excitement—A Negro Welcome — "Miss Belle's Husband"—A Portent— A Sailor's Superstition—Capture—Poor Pat in the Toils—A high-bred General—Lieutenant Adams— A Yankee Provost-Marshal—The Guard-house— —The Restaurant—A Guardsman—Ordered off again—Arrival at Washington.

LAST November it became necessary for me to quit the tranquil shores of England, and make, much to my disgust, a trip across the Atlantic, rendered doubly disagreeable to me by the fact that I was parting for an indefinite period from one whom I loved fondly—my wife, and to whom I had been married but two short months.*

On the Monday afternoon after my arrival I left Boston and proceeded to New York, where I arrived about 11 p.m., and put up at the New York Hotel. I did not sleep here, however, but went over to my mother's residence in Brooklyn almost immediately.

Gaining admittance to the house, and being, as you may suppose, thoroughly conversant with its internal arrangements, I mounted softly on tip-toe to my parents' room and entered. My father, aroused by

---

* These papers were originally intended solely for the perusal of my wife; but, upon second thought, they have been somewhat condensed in material, and have been added to her adventures as an after-piece.

the noise I made—for floors and doors will invariably creak at such times—called out as I opened the door, " Who is that?" "Martin," I replied; for I wished to surprise them as much as possible.

As soon as I had lit the gas I turned upon them and said, " Mother, how do you do?" For the moment she was struck dumb with astonishment, but the next she was in my arms, pressing me to her heart as only a mother can who loves her son devotedly.

We sat for a long time conversing upon many topics—my wife, my future prospects, &c. About three in the morning, however, I left her and retired to my brother's room, who was at the time absent in Boston on business. I do not know why it was, but I felt like a stranger in a strange land; for my heart was with you, over the ocean in merrie England.

All the rest of the night I sat framing a letter to you; and it was late in the morning, just as the faint glimmering streaks of dawn were flashing up from the east, and the distant hum of the city was becoming more and more audible, that I threw myself, tired, weary, and heart-sick, on the bed, and fell asleep to dream of you.

Sleep, did I say? Ay, the sleep that the dog enjoys in his kennel. I think it was about nine in the morning when my mother awakened me. I sprang to my feet, and, hurriedly completing my toilette, descended and entered the dining-room. There was very little said—a monosyllabic breakfast, one of those dismal feasts where Death seems to reign supreme. With me it was soon over; and that same night I was *en route* for Baltimore, bound to

Martinsburg, which I reached, after much delay and detention, after having enjoyed the nervous excitement of running off the track *only twice*, about 6.30 in the evening.

Here I was subjected, with the rest of the passengers, to a strict examination by the Provost-Marshal of my passes and travelling-bag; but finally, after a quarter of an hour's delay, I was allowed to go on.

After passing several sentries and two barricades, I at length found myself at your mother's house. I did not announce my name to any one; but one of the girls rushed up to me, and, after gazing intently at me for a moment, flew out of the room.

Whilst I was revolving over in my mind this inexplicable, to me, scene, she returned, and, half laughing, half in doubt, said, "You's Miss Belle's husband, isn't you?"

I of course assured her that I was. She again disappeared, but returned accompanied by the whole sable household, who, crowding round about me, welcomed me to my home, inquiring affectionately after you, and evidently much disappointed at not finding that you were with me.

Greatly to my chagrin, your mother and sister were at Kennysville, about ten miles distant; but Mrs. G., who could not help shedding tears when she knew who I was, welcomed me as a son. All that evening we sat conversing together; and when, at last, I retired to sleep, it was in your own room; and, as I entered in at the door, I uncovered my head and thought of you.

This was your room; here you had been held a prisoner and had suffered the torture of an agonizing doubt as to your fate. Here lay your books just as you had left them. Writings, quotations, everything to remind me of you was here; and I do not know how long a time I should have stood gazing about me in silence, had it not been for my reverie being disturbed by the little negro servant, who broke the silence by saying, "No one's ever sleep in dis room since Missy Belle been gone—missus says you're de only person as should."

So, when I retired to bed that night, and "Jim" had been dismissed from further attendance upon me, I lay for a long time thinking, looking into the fire, that glimmered and glared about the room, picturing you here, there, and everywhere about the chamber, and thinking of you sadly, far away from me in England—the exile, lonely and sad.

About midnight I fell asleep, and was only aroused from my slumbers late the next morning by Jim, who was making the fire. When I had finished dressing I sat down near the fireplace. I hardly know what persuaded me to do so; but, if you will recollect, on the evening that we parted from one another you placed upon my finger a small diamond-cluster ring,* telling me that there was a peculiar charm attached to it—viz., of forewarning the wearer when in danger by dropping or being taken off. Without thinking, I did the latter.

Now we sailors are somewhat addicted to superstition; and I must confess that I felt a nervous apprehension about myself, which did not leave me despite the endeavours that I made to allay my fears. I told Mrs. G. of the circumstance

* This ring was once the property of an African princess.—B. B. H.

when I met her at breakfast, and she laughed at my credulity; but so firmly was I impressed with the belief, that I already began to feel that I was doomed— a marked man.

And I was. At half-past five—having previously procured a pass—I left for Baltimore; but at Monacocy station I was— judge of my surprise—arrested and kept confined all night under guard as a deserter. As a prisoner, I was of course searched; but, finding nothing upon me, the officer commanding told me that I might retire for the night.

"Where?" I asked.

"Oh! on the floor, by all means," was the response, accompanied with a horse-laugh.

The next day, at my earnest entreaty, I was sent to Point of Rocks, where I was treated more like a dog than a human being; but, fortunately for myself, I was sent on to Harper's Ferry, under a guard of Irish emigrant soldiers, who were far kinder to me than their officers. During the journey they gave me a long history of their wrongs, asserting upon oath that they had been entrapped by the oily tongues of Federal agents in Ireland, who had given them gold and promised them a farm, and two hundred pounds apiece more in gold upon their arrival in the United States, if they would only emigrate for the purpose of tilling the land out West. Upon their arrival in New York, however, they were locked up as prisoners—not allowed to see any one— and were only, after an imprisonment of over three weeks, set free, their liberty having been purchased by their becoming Federal soldiers.

They were also promised eight hundred

dollars bounty and three months furlough, which they had never to this day received, although they had applied for it from time to time; for no sooner had they taken the oath of allegiance than they were sent to the front.

At the conclusion of this narration, which they swore by the "Holy Vargin" was truth and nothing more or less, one of them informed me that they had orders to shoot me if I was *impudint* to them even. "But we won't do it, me bye," they chorussed; "and, if yees says the word, we're yer min to cut over the border with yees."

This, however, was an utter impossibility, for the country was full of Yankee cavalry, looking after Mosby and his men; so I declined their proffered kindness, much to their astonishment and fright, for they begged me for the love of Heaven not to expose them. This I faithfully promised and kept; and, as I bade them good day, just before I was conducted into the presence of General Stephenson, one of them remarked to me, *sotto voce*, "Be my sowl! young fellow, it's too bad to see ye in this condition, when ye ought to be afther mountin' into a saddle."

When ushered into General S.'s room, the General, a grizzly, gray-haired, bearded man, scanned me closely for a short time. After enduring this as long at least as my patience could stand it, I said, "Is there anything remarkable about me, or that you admire?"

"Yes, sir, your duplicity."

"Duplicity?" I reiterated vaguely, seemingly unconscious of the meaning of the word.

"Yes, sir, duplicity: you are a spy, and——"

I interrupted him somewhat sharply, but recollected myself, and held my tongue.

"Where are your papers, passes, despatches?" he asked, angrily.

"Papers I have none, except the 'New York Day-book' and the 'World' of yesterday; despatches—excuse me, did you say despatches?"

"Yes, sir, despatches."

"I'll save you a pun," I remarked, savagely: "I have none. As for my passes, they are there," pointing to a formidable-looking official document that had been brought on with me.

"Ugh!" was the rejoinder to this.

Lieutenant Adams just then made his appearance, and a very nice and gentlemanly fellow he was, too. In striking contrast with the General was his adjutant, the lieutenant.

"You're the husband of Miss Belle Boyd, and you ought to be hung. By the way, we hung one to-day; didn't we, adjutant?"

"What are you going to do?"

"Hang you, if you can't prove your innocence—send you to Washington, perhaps. That will do, sir;" and I left the room.

In a few moments Lieutenant Adams came out, and said, and very kindly too, "Now, Mr. Hardinge, we'll go and get something to eat; and, if I can manage it, you shall sleep elsewhere than in a guard-house. Come into my office for a short time, until I write a letter, and then we will go."

Thanking him for his proffered hospitality, I entered the room and seated myself near the fire—for it was a rainy day, and very disagreeable—and listened with feelings of horror and disgust to the brutal boasts of a braggadocio Provost-Marshal (I wish I could recollect his name, for the sake of humanity), who boasted of having enacted the part of Jack Ketch to a Confederate soldier of "White's Battalion" that very day; remarking, "By ——! didn't the fellow jump when the rope broke!" and he added, "Here's a piece of the rope, young fellow. Wouldn't you like to swing?"

"Not with you, at least, for a hangman," I said; and I did not attempt to suppress my disgust from appearing.

"D—— you! I'll give you a double allowance of dancing on nothing if I do," was the reply.

Shortly after this light and entertaining conversation, Lieutenant Adams and myself left them; and, after a good meal and a short tour about the town, we once more entered his office. But this time I did not stay long; for, although Lieutenant Adams did all in his power to keep me from the guard-house, to that delectable place I went, under the tender auspices of the Provost, who endeavoured to regale me with stories of men that he had "hung."

As for sleeping there, it was out of the question. A terrific fire roared and blazed up the chimney, flinging its heat into a room whose measurement might have been ten feet by twelve. In this space were packed some twenty steaming, drunken soldiers and citizens; and add to this the fact that other animals besides rats and mice were at play in the room, I think you will admit that I was at least uncomfortable.

The next morning, at a later hour, I was allowed to proceed under guard to a very seedy-looking cellar rejoicing in the name of a " Restaurant," where I succeeded in getting some stale oysters and bean coffee. Having finished this delectable breakfast, I was again reminded that I was a prisoner in the Yankees' hands by the sentinel, who carried, in addition to his gun, a watch, and who ostentatiously glanced at it, remarking, as he did so, " Time's up."

" Any news from the front?" I ventured to remark.

" No!"

" Is Mosby in the neighbourhood?"

" I s'pose so."

" How often do the trains go northwards in the course of a day?"

"Twice."

"Corporal," I said, "I am quite an amateur in my way. Come, you have excited my curiosity. Tell me, honestly, now, what you are; for you are the only one of the many soldiers that I have met in my intercourse with the tribe for the last three or four days who is rightly entitled to the name."

He evidently felt flattered, for it was the "Open, Sesame," of his tongue, and he flatly informed me that he was a deserter from the Guards, who had been stationed in Canada. "And I wish to the devil I was back out of the dirty rapscallion set that I've got into. They say birds of a feather flock together; but I'm —— if I am a bird of their stripe."

Our conversation was brought to a close at this period by the door of the guard-house once more being closed upon me. For want of better amusement, I stood watching the farmers or their wives from the country round who came to procure the necessary passes to return to their homes again; and I must confess that the brutal remarks that accompanied the pass, or oftener its refusal, were enough to make the blood of any father, brother, or son boil with indignation.

At 5 p.m., just as I was beginning to despair of ever being sent away from Harper's Ferry, a detective came to me and said, "All humbug; you're the chap, are yer? Come on!"

To this tender appeal I merely said, "I am ready; lead on."

As I passed out he significantly pointed to a six-shooter that was buckled to his side, and remarked, "None o' yer capers."

I could not but help laughing in the fellow's face; and I hardly know what would have been the *finale*, if Lieutenant Adams, who was passing in at that moment, had not said, "Treat him like a gentleman, ———," calling him by his name. And it is to this remark that I, no doubt, am indebted for the little kindnesses I received on my way to Washington.

We arrived in Washington about midnight, and the detective having visited the Provost's office, I was relieved of his further attendance upon me, and at 1 p.m. on Sunday morning I was consigned to a horrible hole known as the Forrest Hall, filled with everything that was infamous, low, and degraded.

CHAPTER X.

Forrest Hall—A Lesson on Prison Luxury—The Torture —Close Packing—The "Neutral Ground"—A goodnatured Sentry—An Aristocrat—"The Gouger"—A tough Contest—Homage to the Victor—An Honour declined — The Carroll Prison — Defacing the Walls—Piety Hall—Unpleasant Tortures—" The Colonel."

FORREST Hall, or, as it is somewhat significantly designated by the fellows who board here at the Government's expense, " The last Ditch," was without exception the most fearful realization of a prison that it was my misfortune ever to have anything to do with: not that I would have you for one moment suppose that I am familiar with a convict's residence; but I have mentioned it merely from the fact that, until I was thus thoroughly convinced to the contrary, I had always entertained the belief that, in this age of improvements and luxury, prisons had been converted by science into luxuriously improvised hotels—watering-places where roughs and rogues retire for a while to recruit their wasting energies.

And in this respect I have always entertained the belief that in America "they know how to manage these things better than in Europe, you know;" but this foretaste of St. Giles and Billingsgate dispelled, and effectively too, any highly coloured and very romantic ideas that I had conceived of prison luxury; and the rose-colour tinting with which I had in fancy painted such residences gave way to a most sombre picture edged with black, that nearly crazed me as I walked gravely backwards and forwards, picking my way daintily through dirty groups of sleeping men or puddles of tobacco-juice with which the floor of this place was saturated.

Situated in Georgetown, on the suburbs of the city of Washington, Forrest Hall was, before the commencement of this devilish struggle, used as a place of public entertainment, where balls and suppers were held or given. A large square-shaped room, it had nothing of beauty to recommend it even then; much less at the present day, when its walls are defaced with unseemly pictures, vulgar writings, or punctured plaster; and even in its halcyon days it was such a room that one felt, however warm one may have been, chilled upon entering.

Four immense windows, reaching from the top almost to the bottom, bound with iron, looked forth upon the street; but none of us ever presumed to gaze from them, for orders were given to shoot dead the audacious wretch who should thus defy the laws. Four others looked out upon what was known as the "Promenade," a small enclosure where we were allowed to walk for half an hour daily. One feature of this "yard," as it was also called, was the hose; an instrument of torture which was applied to "suspects," who were supposed to be deserters from the United States army. Whether it was so or not it was almost impossible to say. The manner of torturing the unfortunate man was after the most approved method of Yankee invention and ingenuity. You may doubtless somewhere have read of the prisoner who was tortured by being fastened in an immovable position beneath a faucet, that permitted to escape, every second, one drop of water, which fell always in one spot upon the forehead, producing a most fearful torture, resulting eventually in insanity. Well, although it was not exactly the same thing, nevertheless it approached it very nearly. For in this instance the victim was made to stand bound securely, to a post, whilst a steady stream of water, whose force was thirty pounds to an inch square, was played upon the small of the back.

It was often the case that the victim, unable to endure the torture, would, guilty or not, give in; and the consequence was, that the authorities, having witnessed the acknowledgment of his crime, would remand him in an exhausted state back to the Hall, to be led out to execution, or conducted to the Penitentiary, to which he would be sentenced for a lifetime.

Again, some, more obdurate and stubborn, would remain firm and unyielding, however fearful the torture, until fainting would ensue, or the medical attendant, who waited in person and watched closely the victim's wrist, would say, "Enough"; when he would be carried back to the room, only to be brought forth to endure the same torture when he had sufficiently recruited his energies to be able to appear once more.

But to revert once more to Forrest Hall. In a space not more than seventy-five feet square were crowded together over five hundred dirty, ragged, and filthy wretches, of all conditions and colour, who had been immured here for many months with the consoling remark, "Your case will be attended to." The dirt that filled the floor was something awful to reflect upon, and here they were obliged to live—here sleep. A space large enough for the promenade of the guards, who were relieved at the end of every four hours, was reserved for them; and whoever the poor wretch was that dared to invade the neutral ground — for such it was called by the residents—he was shot like a dog for his daring; murdered, coolly and deliberately. Right over the entrance to this room was a place called "The Lodge." Here a corporal and three or four sentries are placed, with the same humane orders to execute relative to the shedding of human blood. The place literally swarmed with vermin, and the air is corrupt, and vile with odours that are, at least, to be moderate in one's language, disgusting and nauseating in the extreme.

It was early on a Sunday morning that I entered this sink, after having undergone a rigid examination of my person at the hands of the officers who were quartered at the Hall.

This done, I was handed over to a sergeant, and conducted by him to the room that I have endeavoured to describe to you above. It was so late that (fortunately for me) only some nine or ten out of the whole number that lay huddled together on the floor were awake. One or two stared at me for a short time, but went on again with their play at cards.

A sentry was once more my friend in this place. *He pitied me.* I was glad to have any one's pity, even, for I felt almost like the desperate suicide at times, and the future of my life was enveloped in gloom, so dark and obscure that it was in vain that I attempted to penetrate it.

Having passed the spot where I was standing, wrapped up in my own thoughts, he stopped suddenly, and said, "You surely are not a deserter, sir?"

"You have surmised correctly," I replied.

"What are you doing here, then?" he added, with some surprise.

"That is just what I should like to know myself; and, if you will inform me, I shall thank you for the information."

"An' I suppose you are one of those fellows we call political prisoners; and if you are, by Jove! there's plenty more of your same stripe that would like to have the same information you're after wanting;" and he resumed his beat.

In a short time he came to me, and said, "Why don't you sleep?"

"Sleep!" I said, in astonishment. He grinned at the manner in which I spoke the word *sleep*, and said—

"By ——! there'd only be a clean-picked skeleton of you in the morning."

"Then I will try to fancy myself on the quarter-deck for four hours;" and I commenced to promenade up and down with the sentry, and it was not until late the next morning that I gave up, and was forced to sit down; but I first took my handkerchief and brushed away the dirt on the floor as well as I could before I did so.

As the morning wore on apace, the rascals, who by this time were thoroughly awake, came and stared at me, or asked me questions of myself, business, &c. To the former I affected a perfect indifference, but to the latter I kept my tongue, which brought down innumerable left-handed blessings from these fellows, who saw in me, as they did not abstain from informing their comrades, "a —— aristocrat."

Taking my silence for fear, they became bolder. One of them, a wall-eyed, villainous scoundrel, knocked my hat off. Picking it up, I replaced it on my head without apparently noticing the offender. Growing bolder, the cries of "Toss him! toss the swell cove! mash him! jam him!" were raised on all sides. A blanket was getting stretched for my special benefit, and I determined to act instantaneously.

Near the stove was a goodly sized stick

of wood, that was used for supporting the door when opened. I determined to get possession of it; so I walked up quietly, and, gaining possession of the instrument that was soon to decide my fate, I retreated to a corner, and waited for them.

It was not long. A party advanced, and then halted, when the wall-eyed man, who was known as "the Gouger"—a name that he had won from his prowess in tearing the eyes from out the sockets of others— came as near as was prudently safe, for I swung the stick defiantly as he advanced, and said—

"Now, young 'un, if yer don't give in, I'll bite yer nose off. Come, now, are yer goin' to?"

To his tender and merciful intentions as regarded my nose I paid no attention.

"Oh, yer ain't agoin' to, then, are yer? Well, I'll have a fresh-meat breakfast, by ——! this morning, at any rate. Come on, bullies."

I only remember one thing until the whole affair was over; and this is the picture: "the Gouger" and his second advancing as I swung my trusty weapon in a circle about me, the pointed edge of the stick cutting into the bridge of "the Gouger's" nose, and effectually closing an eye for him, and the remaining force of the blow being received by his second on the temple, who fell like a lump of lead by his leader. Then it was that I sprang forward, slashing right and left as I went; but there was no necessity to do murder, for they gave way before me; and the sentry, who had been watching the battle, received me with the remark, as I gained his side, panting from the exertion, " By ——! if I hadn't have liked you, I'd have shot you for mutiny; but you did that well: they won't trouble you any more, I'll bet."

Nor did they. On the contrary, a "select committee," to my great surprise, waited upon me about 10 a.m., and their spokesman informed me that by a unanimous vote I had been chosen their president, and, if I would accept the leadership of "the Owls," it was at my command.

To their astonishment, I refused them; but, not wishing to make them my enemies, for I had no idea how long I was to remain here, I did so as politely as possible.

Fortunately for me, in the afternoon I was sent for; and, under guard, I was conveyed to the Provost-Marshal's office, in Washington City. Here I was kept for over an hour, in a place that was partitioned off for rebels, a ferocious-looking aspirant for military honours guarding me the while. Several of the clerks, who had ascertained from their superior who I was, attempted to converse with me, but in this they failed most decidedly.

Shortly after this I was taken, under the surveillance of Captain —— and four of his satellites, to the Old Capitol. On my way to that place I was kindly permitted to partake of some food—the first that I had eaten for over twenty-four hours—at "Hanmack's," and to the proprietor of that place I was indebted for much attention.

I then resumed my journey once more,

after running " a muck," so to speak, of the curious loungers, for the churches were fast pouring forth their inmates upon the street, and the terrific fire of conversation from the Captain, which was by far the worst torture I had to endure.

On my arrival at the Old Capitol I was welcomed by a one-armed lieutenant, who had " seen servin'," but when he did not say, and whom I ascertained to belong to that body of men known as the " invalid corps." I was ordered to sit down, and, after a running fire of questions, I was sent off to the Carroll Prison, under the guard of two soldiers.

I was not long in reaching it, for the political bastile is situated not far from its prototype, the Old Capitol. I was received by the under-superintendent, who, having registered my name, age, occupation, height, business, ancestry, &c., was good enough to relieve me of some money—not all, for I had been deprived of most by " the gallant knights of the greenwood," through whose merciless fingers I did not pass unscathed, and who certainly have a taking way about them. A diminutive penknife which was also " captured," although I begged to retain it as a favour, was refused on the plea that I might injure myself.

This over, I was conducted to Room No. 35, to keep company with a spy and a blockade-runner. On its walls, rudely executed with a piece of charred wood, I wrote our names, one day, and drew above them the English and Confederate flags, which, coming under notice of the sentinel outside, drew down upon my devoted head a whole mouthful of curses, loud and deep. Some wag, a previous inmate of this room, had written, *à la* Jack Sheppard, over the door the following very curious misnomer: "Piety Hall!" "Piety Hall" is certainly a most deplorable spot. Four bunks, filled with bedding of a most suspicious character, occupy one-third of the space. I very foolishly slept in one of these "beds," as they are designated here, but I can assure you that I regretted it exceedingly long before morning.

It was almost an utter impossibility to tell the time correctly in this place, for the window that opened on a passage-way without is so completely enclosed with the cell that has evidently been added to the building since the commencement of the war, and which is reserved exclusively for "close confinement," that it is not until a very late hour in the forenoon that daylight favours us with its presence at all. A stove in the centre of the room is used by us to cook whatever we choose to buy from the sutler, Mr. Donelly, who has had the monopoly of this prison since the beginning of the rebellion.

The morning after my arrival at the Carroll, in company with the blockade-runner, I descended into the yard, when, after refreshing myself with a hearty wash at the pump, I entered the *salle à manger* for my breakfast. I could eat nothing. The coffee is a mixture of—but I will not attempt to describe it—whilst the "hard tack," as the old inmates call it, is the flintiest kind of flour that was ever baked and honoured with the appellation of biscuit. So I walked out into the yard, and strolled listlessly about, wondering, as prisoners will, when I should be released.

About 11 a.m. I again went up to my room, and received from the sentinel a reprimand for remaining below in the yard, accompanied with the remark that "if I didn't mind my eye, I'd have old Wood after me."

One of my room-mates said, "What was that old fool saying?"

I repeated the above remark to him, when they both laughed derisively and said, "Don't you believe all they tell you: if you do, you will have a surfeit of gasconade and a troublesome indigestion."

The second day after my arrival the "Colonel" entered the room and said, "Ho, ho, here we are! So you're the husband of the famous Belle Boyd, are you? Well, we haven't got her, but we've got her husband, that's next to it;" and before I had time to reply he was out of the room;

and this was the way that I first made the acquaintance of William P. Wood, the superintendent of the Old Capitol and Carroll.

CHAPTER XI.

Journal continued—Letter to Mr. Stanton—Visit from Judge Turner—Room 25—An Introduction in due form—Pleasant Society—A Dinner at last—Good Advice—A clandestine Communication—False Alarm—"That reminds me of a good Story" A Massachusetts Officer in Trouble—The " Smasher's " Sentence—An imprisoned Wife and Child—Blockade-running.

5th December.—Having procured some paper from the sutler, I wrote to Mr. Stanton with a simple statement of my case.

This document I forwarded to Judge

Turner, who *attends* to all the cases of the prisoners held here. That gentleman, after the expiration of three days, sent for me; and having asked me, in the presence of witnesses, if I had written it, to which I answered in the affirmative, then swore me as to the truthfulness of it, and dismissed me from his awful presence, with the assurance that he would attend to it in the proper course of time.

I shall not readily forget my introduction to the inmates of Rooms 25 and 26, to which I was now transferred. I was introduced into my new quarters by Captain Mark T. "Gentlemen," he said, " allow me to introduce to this select and distinguished company, Lieutenant S. Wilde Hardinge, formerly of the United States navy, now of England, but just at present boarding with the freemen of the city at the Old Carroll Prison." (A momentary pause.) "Allow me, sir—Captain McD., of Pennsylvania, a counterfeiter, sir; brought here not for an attempt to counterfeit himself, but for the crime of counterfeiting United States green-backs, and buying Southern horses with them." "Mr. Parker, sir" (as I was somewhat unceremoniously pushed round in front of him), "a blacksmith, not of anvils, but of the city of Brotherly Love, a forger by trade. He was brought up at the forge; and how could such an apt scholar end otherwise than in forging the United States Government?" "Ah, H." (familiarly), "two distinguished 'colonels' from New York, charged with ballot-box stuffing, and having the presumption to vote for McClellan; a bad case, sir, I assure you, as they [the authorities] keep putting their trial off for further evidence, which they cannot procure. However, they have an idea that they are sulky, and so they intend to keep them here. Ah, sir, this is a glorious country; nothing like it; in fact, a country whose institutions one ought to esteem, for they hang you first, and try you afterwards."

Captain T. having finished his somewhat lengthy harangue, I ventured to remark, "And what, sir, may I ask, is your crime?" "Ah! mine," said he, winking complacently, "is *nothing!* but, as out of nothing came something, I presume they'll make it out of my case."

Here the introduction suddenly ceased; for, dinner being announced, every one rushed for a seat, and devoured, somewhat ravenously, it must be confessed, everything, excepting what was not eatable, upon the table; an example which I was not slow to imitate, for it had been over two weeks since I had the good fortune to get a mouthful of anything really eatable.

December 7th.—I woke up very early this morning, and, having dressed myself, strolled about the yard below for a while in conversation with two or three others incarcerated here—for nothing; at least, that is the invariable answer.

By way of an explanation of this, one of them said to me, "It don't do, Mr. H., to know too much in a place like this. You are a new comer: let me advise you to ask no questions, and answer fewer. I don't mean to say there are spies here, but I wouldn't trust my own father in here;" and, having finished his sentence, he left me.

I can see the ladies in the different

rooms in that portion of the building devoted to them, gazing down, through their iron bars, into the yard, upon the prisoners, who are allowed to walk about here at stated intervals. I accomplished the prison feat of exchanging notes with a "close-confined" prisoner, an exploit which was executed when the Hessian sentry had his back turned upon us, and which would have been punished with bread and water in the guard-house for forty-eight hours, had it been discovered.

It is quite worthy of notice that one seems to take an indescribable pleasure in eluding the vigilance of the sentries at all times, not so much for any particular reason, but merely for the purpose of passing away the time, and proving that such a thing can be done in spite of the "Rules and Regulations."

Captain Marsh left Room 26 to-day. He had been prisoner here for some time, but eventually was released without a trial or any satisfaction being accorded to him. His arrest was very ingeniously managed, Secretary Stanton ordering him to report for examination for Colonel at Washington. Captain M. was " at the front," *i.e.*, before Richmond, when he received this mandate; but judge of his surprise when, upon his arrival, instead of being promoted, he was ordered to the Carroll, and detained there.

December 9th.—This evening, as we were seated conversing or playing cards, for want of some better occupation, we were somewhat startled by the cry of " Officer of the keys! corporal of the guard! Post No. 7!" and almost simultaneously with it came the report of a musket, that sent whist-players and every one else to their feet. Officers and men rushed to their different stations, and the general belief, for the moment, was that some one had been shot in attempting to escape. Such, however, was not the case; it proving to be only the accidental discharge of a fire-arm, through the carelessness of a sentinel who had just come off post, and was placing his piece in the rack, when it fell, the jar causing it to go off. The ball passed upwards through the floor, going through a bed in 26, but fortunately without wounding its inmate. This is not the first instance of this kind that has occurred.

Said Colonel Wood, who at that time was playing Inspector of the rooms, " That reminds me of a good story." The *good story* was as follows:—

" There was a fellow, an officer in the

Confederate States Army, who received some money from a lady who was held in my residence for stubborn people. With this he bribed the sentinel who was in the yard beneath to let him attempt an escape. The sentinel agreed; but I got wind of the affair an hour before it took place; and, walking up to the sentinel, I said, 'Now, you —— ——, I've got you in my power; and, if you don't shoot that —— rebel, I'll have you hung." So when Mr. Rebel gets out of the window, Mr. Sentinel blazes away at him, and down he drops kerflummuxed."

"What became of him?" asked one of his audience.

"Why, —— him, he died in the hospital several days afterwards."

December 11*th*.—A captain in the Massachusetts 8th was sent into 26 to-day.

He had been arrested and imprisoned in the Baltimore Gaol for six weeks. In about an hour after his appearance amongst us he was ordered out, and put into close confinement.

Captain McD., an incarcerated prisoner in 26, received the news of his sentence of court-martial through the "Star" of this evening. He was convicted of passing counterfeit money, and was sentenced to ten years' imprisonment in the Clinton Prison, New Jersey, has been cashiered the service, and disqualified from holding any office of honour, trust, and profit under the United States Government, and to pay a fine of $5000 : this latter item, fortunately for him, is in " green-backs."

He is a stout-built, thick-set, brawny-looking man, with black eyes and hair, and has lost a finger in the service of the Union. I watched his countenance closely as his eyes met the paragraph containing his sentence. Every one had seen it, but none cared to break the intelligence. He gave a sudden spasmodic start, and sat for as much as ten minutes gazing at it. How he must have felt inwardly at that time none can know but himself. It made one feel cold and nervous to see him sit there so quietly. Ten years! a lifetime for him. His hopes for the future were blighted. Farewell for him to all life's charms: he is dead henceforth and for ever to the world. I would not have been in his place for thousands.

There he sat, without moving, and Room 26 was very quiet, for the occupants of it were looking at him. He evidently and suddenly became aware of this fact, and, looking up from the fatal "Star," he said, "I'm in for it. They've done for me. Well, ten years imprisonment! Humph!" (and he laughed), "I'm glad of that: I'll get out sooner." Then he got up and walked out of the room, and we all of us somehow felt relieved when he had gone.

December 15th.—Glancing up at the windows of Room 40, I saw this afternoon, whilst walking up and down the yard, a poor little child—a girl—about four years old, and standing close beside her was her mother. She clasped the iron bars of the window with childish glee, and did not seem to be aware that the cold, repelling touch of the iron that encircled her present abode was that of prison bars, that held her captive from the outer world. Her merry little laugh was truly painful to listen to.

"Aunt Lizzie" was in the sutler's at this time, so I asked her who it was.

"Who dat lady, massa? Dat's Mrs. K."

"What is her crime?" I asked.

"Oh, her husband was drafted, and she connived at his escape out ob de country, so they arrested her; an' now she's drefful feared that he'll guv hisself up in her place."

December 17*th*.—The ladies in Room 42 sent me a note, smuggled by ——, in which they thanked me for presents, at different times, of wine and delicacies for the table, that I had procured; for I have followed the business of blockade-runner very successfully since I have been in here: no matter if I have ill-luck for an attendant outside in that dashing and very exciting business.

December 20*th.*—I cannot imagine why I can hear no news of you. Mr. Wood says, "You are very foolish, Mr. H., to fret: everything is fair in love and war;" so I am forced to construe out of the latter portion of his sentence that others are employed in reading my letters. What a jolly thing military surveillance is!

CHAPTER XII.

Introduced to the Ladies' Ward—Colonel Wood and his "Reminiscence-book"—Interview with Judge Turner—Sherman's Officers in Georgia—A hideous Outrage—Christmas in Prison—Home-sick—A drunken Sentry—Another Visit to the Ladies—The Young Girl's Sick Bed—A Rough Prison Carol.

December 21st.—I was introduced to the ladies in 42 to-day, and spent a very pleasant half-hour in their society; and so quickly did the time slip away, that I was only reminded that the thirty minutes were gone by the officer of the keys, who, looking at his watch, said, "Time's up!" Mrs. Colonel M. spoke of you, and said "that you were undeniably the pet of the Confederacy, and would always be looked upon as its child as long as the Confederacy existed and had a name."

December 23rd.—No signs of my being released yet. Mrs. Colonel M. remarked, and in the presence of Mr. Wood, to-day, "I have material enough of Bastile life, as exemplified in my treatment here, for a book."

"Mrs. M.," said Wood, and he laughed, "no one will ever be able to write a truthful account of the Capitol and Carroll Prisons. I have a reminiscence-book, where I put everything that occurs of note within these walls. If published, it would equal any of Reynolds' novels of the Tower of London."

Then he spoke of Mrs. Horns. "I did that girl an injustice. By ——! she was no traitor to the South. It was I who got the papers that condemned her friends, without her knowledge and consent; and Mrs. G., when she went to Richmond, ruined and completely crushed her." Turning to Mrs. Colonel M., he added, "You may believe me or not, but Mrs. G. used to write me notes, until I fairly got sick of her, and afterwards she came out with a vengeance against me. But, as I rather glory in my origin, it didn't hurt me."

December 24th.—My poor mother-in-law, in a letter to me to-day, says, "What have I done, a weak, defenceless woman, weighed down with sorrow and care, that that they will not permit me to come on to Washington and see you?"

Had an interview with Judge **Turner** in

the afternoon. Judge Turner, *loquitur*, his back to the fire, hat over his eyes (probably from very shame), a cigar in his mouth:—

"Good morning, Mr. H."

"Good afternoon, sir."

"Your business, Mr. H.?"

"This, sir: can you inform me when I am to be released?"

"Oh, one of these days."

"Are there any charges against me?"

"None, sir; that is, perhaps there may be."

"Then why am I held prisoner here?"

"Because it pleases the Government."

"Ah! but do you call it justice?"

Judge Turner (frowning):—"Be very careful what you say, sir. You are held here because it pleases Mr. Stanton; besides, your wife won't destroy any more of our army than she has done, Mr. H., if you are held as a hostage; and Mr. Stanton has an affectionate regard for your future welfare."

What could I do? I was like the mouse, a prisoner in the cage, and at the mercy of the lion.

"I repeat my question," I said: "is it justice?"

"Justice or not," said that worthy judge, "we keep you here to make a patriot of you."

Mr. M. told me to-day two stories: one of them was of Sherman's march through Georgia. Mrs. M—— was tied to her chair and flogged, her clothes first being stripped to her waist. Leather straps were used for the purpose. A negro informed the officer that her husband had buried $20,000 in gold, and that she was aware of its hiding-place; so, finding that threats could not extort the secret, they used force.

As she stood there writhing in her agony, she appealed to the fellow, who was a "Capting," for mercy; but the ruffianly scoundrel's only reply was, "D—n you: tell us where the gold is hid, and I'll let you up." But this she could not do, and the infuriated wretches continued until she fainted, and the brutes then left her.

The other story was this, and not the less worthy of comment as it came from the lips of a lady, both in position, as regarded her standing in society, and in wealth and accomplishments. I have no reason to urge you not to publish it to the world. Near the Rio Grande a Mrs. —— lived quietly and undisturbed, though the civil war raged about her, until a band of these "patriots for the restoration of the Union" took possession of the place for a few hours. Several of them entered her house in the night-time and ascended to her room, where she lay sick with rheumatism and unable to move. Her servant, a young quadroon, who was waiting upon her, concealed herself in the bed; but she was dragged from her hiding-place, and these less than men, rendered furious with drink, and in the presence of the agonized and terrified lady, and in spite of her protestations and appeals for mercy, committed upon the unhappy girl the worst of outrages.

Christmas Eve.—About nine p.m. I sat down to a game of cards, and I am sorry to say that it lasted far into the morning—Sunday morning, and Christmas too; but you must excuse me, for you know that I was a prisoner. I retired to my bed about four a.m., and fell asleep almost immediately, waking up with the winter sun streaming into my face, unwell and low-spirited.

In "our room," 25, hangs, suspended from the ceiling, an evergreen wreath, with two figures pendant from it, the only thing here, in this dismal place, to recall to one's mind Christmas, save that the bells are already beginning to ring out merrily. No greetings from those you love meet your ears. Some few bid you "Merry Christmas," as you pass them by; but the look which accompanies it is low and melancholy, betokening that the one who gives the "God's greeting" says so mechanically.

Egg-nog has already commenced to flow

freely in our room. Mr. Donelly's shop is much patronized this morning for whiskey and weiss-beer (the latter drink decidedly doctored, and a late importation, I should judge), eggs, and other necessaries that he doles forth for money, to us. A glorious day, yet every one is down-hearted. I chew the bitter cud of reflection as I smoke my cigar.

Many of my fellow-prisoners have already drowned their sorrows in drink. An occasional maudlin carol comes from the barred window of some caged bird. As the day wears on apace, so does the state of intoxication increase. The sentries are maudlin, the prisoners noisy or sullen as the liquor which they have drunk may affect them. Several are insulting. Without, drunken men and women reel through the streets. Why should I grumble, after all? There is misery and sorrow without, in this world, as well as within. I have not smiled to-day, but two or three times my eyes have been filled with tears; for I have been thinking of you, Belle, a stranger in a strange land, waiting sad and lonely for my return.

So the day creeps slowly along. The sentries are drunk, and many of the prisoners are dozing off, the effects of whiskey, made up of morphene and other slow poisons.

A few moments ago one of the sentries asserted his authority with me.

Sentry (intoxicated):— " Say! where in the —— are you going to?" crossing his gun before me at the same moment.

" Are you addressing your conversation to me?" I ask.

" I don't want none of your ——

palaver. Get back into that room, or I'll shoot you."

I could stand this no longer; but I folded my arms, and, looking him straight in the eyes, I said, "I am unarmed. Shoot if you dare; but, by Heaven! if you miss me, I shall not you."

The muzzle of his piece dropped, and, as I walk away, three cheers are given for me by the prisoners who were witnesses of the affair.

Several of the inmates of Carroll Prison have been locked up in their rooms for being noisy; cheering for Jeff. Davis and the Southern Confederacy, and groaning for Sherman and Governor Brown, of Georgia.

Dinner is announced at last: goose, and turkey, and mince-pies for Room 26; bean-soup and bread for the other prisoners. The former dinner passed off in silence. Every mouthful one takes seems like lead. Nobody laughs or smiles: some few curse and swear.

The dinner is over. At the latter every one scowls, grumbles, or swears, and leaves the room—the *salle à manger* of the Carroll Prison—chewing, by way of dessert, "hard tack."

I ask permission to see the ladies in 42. Wood is gracious to-day, and the request is granted, and for a few brief minutes I feel differently. Suddenly, with a bang, the door is flung open. In rushes Wood, utterly regardless of the poor sick girl who lies writhing with pain upon her bed —the same bed in which you slept, in the same room; and fancy made me always picture you as the sufferer, as you suffered here months before—and roars out in his loudest tones as he discourses upon Atheism, then off, before you are quite sure that you have not made up your mind to knock him down, or show him the door.

As I stood in No. 42 this afternoon, despite myself, the tears sprang to my eyes. There, on the bed, lay poor Miss Mollie McDonough, groaning and moaning with pain, sick and delirious; for close imprisonment had, with its iron grasp, taken hold upon her delicate frame, and, after a brief struggle, she had succumbed before it.

"The doctor says she must be removed," whispers Mrs. Colonel M. to me.

"Why, then, is it not done?" I rejoin.

"Because that renegade Virginian refuses to let it be done."

Poor Mollie! I thought of you, Belle,

as I gazed upon her this evening, and the blood rushed to my temples, and I clenched my hands in silent wrath.

Mrs. Colonel M. tells me that Wood rushed into the room this morning, and yelled out at the top of his voice, "Hooray, Mollie! I've got your father a prisoner." She gave one shriek, and cried out in her agony, "My God! what will become of my poor mother now?"

Pretty scene! pretty language was that, to be used in a sick girl's room! Mrs. Colonel M., who had stood by, a silent witness of the scene, said to Mr. Wood, "For God's sake, sir, do you want to finish your work by killing her?"

"Madam, you can't ride a high horse here." "No, sir," said Mrs. M.; "I leave that for Mr. Wood to do." Bang went the door, and he was gone, and in a few minutes he returned with Mr. McDonough.

It was at muster-roll in the evening I left for Room 25, where Colonel Wood was, swearing as usual, and holding forth upon some argument that was engrossing the attention of a crowd of tobacco-smokers lying on the beds in every conceivable position; a choice party for Sunday evening; and, in their intercourse with one another, oaths made up what their ideas lacked in the formation of their sentiments.

Finally Wood sang a song. Give him his due: he sang it well and with feeling. Then he left us, for which I fervently thanked Heaven. The moment that he went out singing commenced. Every one who could not sing was compelled to make a speech, and in this manner we managed to pass the time away quickly. When it came to my turn to sing, I gave them the following verses, which I had hastily written for the occasion; and, as I went on, one by one, the members who formed the company of Rooms 25 and 26 joined in the strain, until every one who could sing had done their part to swell the volume of song; and, at its conclusion, long applause greeted me from all sides. The following was the song, sung to the tune of "God save the Queen:"—

I.

" ' Land of the Pilgrims' pride,
 Land where our fathers died,'
  Thy doom is read.
From every hill and glen,
In lowland, marsh, and fen,
Thy fate is written there,
  Thy glory fled.

II.

" Ambition holds her sway;
 Injustice rules the day.

Save us, O God!
Spies, paid by those who reign,
Belie the freeman's fame,
And terror reigns supreme.
Help us, good Lord!

• • •

IV.

" Arise, ye men who dare,
Who for your rights 'do care :'
Uphold the laws.
Uphold them as they were,
Not as at present are :
Prove freemen as of yore.
Uphold your cause.

V.

" What! are ye silent still?
Have ye no manly will
To battle them ?
Yes, yes! ye will, ye come :
I hear the fife and drum !
Hark to th' increasing hum
Of fearless men.

VI.

" Strike ! for the old times gone.
Strike ! for your slaughtered sons,

> And honour fled.
> Down with the feudal horde,
> Who irritate and goad,
> With prison, debt, and sword,
> And scoff the dead."

You know that I do not claim to be a poet; so that should you, in glancing over these scraps, have your attention directed for a moment to their errors, forbear, if you please, from laughing at them, and recollect that they were thrown off hastily in my prison home, and served to while away a few heavy moments on Christmas evening.

CHAPTER XIII.

Mr. H.'s Journal continued—A Visit from my Parents—The Order for Removal—On the March—"Do you know Belle Boyd?"—An abrupt Introduction—Arrival in Philadelphia—Dismal Night Quarters—An unpleasant Ordeal—The Menagerie—*En route* for Wilmington—An Eight-mile March—The *Osceola*—Fort Delaware—"Fresh Fish"—"Miss Belle Boyd's Husband"—New Year's Eve—Turned Cook—Snowballing—Sharp Practice.

On the 30th day of December, as I was busily engaged in writing, Mr. Wilson, the superintendent, called me down into the office to see my father and mother, who had come on from New York to visit me.

Previous to their coming to the Old Carroll they had gone to Secretary Stanton to procure the necessary pass. That gentleman · expressed himself astonished at their coming, but, after some considerable delay, having ascertained that the purport of their visit was purely such an one as two fond parents would be supposed to pay their son in "durance vile," gave them the necessary order, without which they could not have seen me.

Whilst we were seated together, conversing upon various topics, Mr. Wilson entered the room and said, addressing his remarks to me—

"Mr. Hardinge, you must get ready, sir."

"For what?" I said. "Is it then indeed true that I am to be sent to Fort Delaware?"

"I presume so, sir," was the reply to my inquiry.

Of course I was powerless to do aught for myself to prevent it. The scene that ensued was very affecting. My poor mother wept bitterly, and, unable to endure it unmoved any longer, I hastily quitted the room.

Whilst engaged in packing together what few articles of clothing I possessed —I do not imagine I was more than five minutes about it—I was again interrupted by Mr. Wilson with—

"Come, sir!"

"But I have not got my things together yet," I said.

"Well, if you haven't, there ain't no time to spare; so come along with you."

Seeing no possible way of obtaining a brief respite, I hastily bid adieu to those of my room-mates who were about me, and, taking my few clothes, I followed my gaoler.

Down-stairs my poor mother again saw me; she was still weeping, and at times sobbed audibly. Near her, my father stood looking at me sadly.

My mother pressed forward and flung her arms round my neck, saying as she did so, "God bless you, my son!" and then, blinded by her tears, she staggered rather than walked from the room, my father following.

I was immediately searched, then gruffly ordered to "Fall in and be d——d to you!" with the rest of the prisoners, seven in number.

The orders were then given to "Right

face! Forward, march!" and away we went. In front of this modern bastile we were again halted. Guards were then stationed on each side of us, a lieutenant marching in front with a drawn sword.

We were, upon our arrival at the dépôt, again halted and drawn up into line, where we remained for some time, the rain descending upon us in torrents, drenching us to the skin. We asked permission of our guards to seek shelter under a roof where they themselves were standing, but we were gruffly refused.

When the rain had ceased we were marched into one of the railway-carriages. Lieutenant C., belonging to Major Harry Gilmore's command, sat on the same seat with me. He was, as I afterwards found, very loquacious, and, though a perfect stranger, entered into a spirited conversation that was kept up nearly the whole way. As I have before stated, he did not, of course, know who *I* was, nor my name; and once, during a lull in our discussions, he said—

"By the way, did you ever hear tell of Miss Belle Boyd?"

I smilingly assented that I had.

"Well," he said, "there isn't a Southerner who would not lay down his life for her. When I was at the battle of Winchester I was wounded, and she came into the hospital where I was and inquired if there were any Maryland boys there. Amongst other delicacies, she gave me some very nice peach-brandy. She and Mrs. G. were in the fort, if I err not, cheering us on when we made a charge and drove the Yankees back. When she was in Montgomery

Hall, Alabama, in 1863, she attended a ball held there, and was *the* belle. She stopped a duel between two Frenchmen who were going to fight in the garden attached to the hotel. When she came back from her imprisonment she brought me a splendid uniform. 'You have no idea how every one loves and respects her," he added; "however, she married a Yankee, so I understand. But Miss Belle would never marry a Yankee I am certain; I'll bet he was a rebel: indeed, I am confident of it; and——"

"And the gentleman who sits beside you is her husband," I added, interrupting him; "and, like yourself, sir, I am a prisoner held by the Yankees."

I never in my life saw a person so thoroughly dumfounded and confused for the moment; but finally he said—

"Well, I trust that you will pardon me for what I have said; upon my honour I did not know who you were, or I would never have done as I have."

"You have said nothing," I replied, "that a gentleman could construe into an insult; and I am happy to make the acquaintance of one who knew my wife so well." And for the rest of the way we were the best of friends.

We arrived in Philadelphia about midnight; the same systematic process of guarding us was gone through with, and as we were marched out of the carriages sleepy passengers rubbed their eyes and stared at the "Johnnies" as we passed by them. We were quickly moved over opposite the station. Here we were halted for a few moments, the lieutenant leaving us in charge of the sergeant whilst he went off to gather further information in regard to our movements. He returned, however, in a few moments; and, again taking up our line of march, we filed to the left, then to the right, in through a gateway, under an arch, through what had once been a doorway, then down through a long corridor whose sides were filled with camp bedsteads, and finally a dismal slave-pen, where there were no windows, only a narrow grated door. This, we were informed, was to be our quarters for the night. Our beds were the hard boards, our coverings what we stood in, our pillows knapsacks or valises.

Sleep was out of the question; so, for the consideration of ten dollars in "greenbacks" (about two pounds sterling), I purchased from a calculating specimen of

Yankeedom about *tenpence* worth of tobacco, and tried to drown my cares and sorrows by smoking; but, although the "smoke" vanished, my woes and sorrows still clung to me. I felt very sore, stiff, cross, out of temper, and indisposed every way, which was in a measure increased the next morning by a breakfast off tin ware, of *something*. I know that I was very hungry, and ate and drank it.

Could any one be more miserable than we under the circumstances? Soldiers, sailors, flunkies, women, &c., came and stared at us.

"So that is him! oh my!" was the sentiment of a very stout, red-faced woman, staring in upon me. "Who'd a-thought it of him? What a wicked man!"

"What will they do with him?" I heard one ask of another.

"Oh, hang him," was the fellow's reply.

"Roasting's too good for him," said the other, with a laugh.

"I wonder if I can get a button or piece of his coat?" I heard some one else say.

"Ask him," said another.

This species of degrading torture I endured until noon-time; when we were ordered out, and conducted, still under guard, to the cars that we had occupied the night before on our way from Washington, now on our way to Wilmington, Delaware, where we arrived in about two hours' time.

Once more we were ordered out of the carriage. I obeyed the command with an apathetic listlessness, for I had lost all spirit, as had the rest of our party, two of whom were old gentlemen, men who, already had one foot in the grave, political prisoners like myself, men who had refused to take the oath of allegiance to the United States Government.

This time we had a journey of eight miles on foot to make. True, apparently, this was not long; but to us it was indeed so. The roads were very bad; and almost all of the way we were over our ankles in mud and slushy snow; and it was not until after three hours of this torture that we marched into Newcastle. As we passed through the principal street women and men rushed to the windows and doors to see us, whilst a guard of honour (?), extemporized from all the small boys and girls in the village, attended us in the front and rear, gazing at us in wonderment.

Arriving at the steamboat landing, much to our disappointment and surprise, the steamer was not to be found, and we were ordered to right about; and this time, as if to add insult to injury, we were conducted to the Newcastle gaol, and confined in a convict's cell.

In this horrid place we were left to our meditations until far into the evening, when we were marched out; and this time it was with a sensation of relief that I passed on to the deck of the *Osceola*. About 8 p.m. the *Osceola* got under way and proceeded down the river, *en route* for the fortress, about twelve miles distant. Several officers stationed at that place were on board, and came aft, questioning us, scanning our attire, features, &c.; and, in fact, doing everything but poke us with sticks to make us roar.

Upon our arrival at the landing (about 10 p.m.) the same routine of guarding was gone through with as I have before described. At last we reached the provost-marshal's office. Here our names were registered, our age, State, when born, profession, whether citizen or soldier, &c.; and, this accomplished, it being late, we were conducted into the "Privates' Barracks," and lodged in the Virginia division, in which were confined some thirteen hundred privates—a place that a gentleman-farmer in this country would not have permitted his pigs to live in, much less human beings.

As we entered the doorway yells and shouts from every side greeted us of "Fresh fish! fresh fish!" Men and boys crowded around us to find out from "whence we came," "what we were held for," "who we were," and last, but not least, "had they gone through us;" in other words, and more plainly speaking, "had the sentries outside searched us."

To this last question I assured my questioners that the Yankees outside had done so most effectually.

Several of them proposed "tossing us in a blanket," by way of diversion to the rest, and many were evidently in favour of it, when suddenly Sergeant B—— of the division sprang forward and shouted out at the top of his voice—

"By Jove! boys, this gentleman is Miss Belle Boyd's husband; you wouldn't wound her feelings by insulting him, would you?"

In an instant the shout that was raised was perfectly deafening. I was received with *empressement* by the whole body of Confederate prisoners.

In spite of this, however, I passed a

miserable night, and awoke more dead than alive with the excessive cold, having no covering to shield me from the weather, the hard floor for my bed. At 9 a.m I ate my initiatory meal at Fort Delaware, consisting of a piece of flinty bread and the smallest morsel of pork, yellow with age. The latter delicacy I gave away, not having been here long enough to appreciate such dainties and eat anything that was placed before me.

Jan. 1st, 1865.—I passed a dreadful New Year's Eve; cowering over the fire until far into the mid-watch, with my gloomy thoughts for sole companions—fitting company, though, for such a place as this. The floor is my bed again to-night, and I sleep as the dogs sleep—half-waking, half-sleeping. Once I awoke, hearing some one engaged in prayer; deep silence prevailed round about; and whoever he was—the speaker I mean—he spoke impressively. Before I retired for the night I called upon General Vance and his staff, and passed a very pleasant evening.

Jan. 2nd.—Some of the "boys" gave me a blanket, and another handed me his overcoat; so that I managed to sleep warmer than usual. Found several friends of mine here from Mobile, Alabama. Captain W. gave me a very good cup of coffee for my dinner. The days drag wearily by, God knows. Everybody treats me kindly. I have found warm friends. Am getting accustomed to my "feather bed of boards."

Jan. 2nd.—Two letters. Very gloomy, and dull, and cold. In the evening heard some very fine singing; Captain —— sang an aria from "Norma" that he rendered excellently well.

Jan. 3rd and 4th.—Wrote to my friends outside the prison to-day. Whilst engaged in this occupation, one of General Vance's aides brought me an invitation from the General to dine with them. Passed a pleasant afternoon in their society; and was introduced to Captain M., brother of General M., the distinguished Kentucky cavalry officer, and we became very warm friends afterwards.

Jan. 5th.—I attempted my first cup of tea this morning. Just fancy my having turned cook! My friends laughed heartily at my handiwork; *for I put the tea in the cup, then the snow upon that*, waiting for that to melt into water and boil. Meanwhile the tea suffered the natural result of such stupidity by being burnt.

Jan. 6th.—Saw an account in the paper of my friend Mrs. Col. —— having been sent South. Thank God she is free!

Jan. 8th.—Received a letter from one of my friends outside to-day, smuggled in by the underground route; there is hope for me yet in Rome with Nero. Saw an account of my removal from the Carroll Prison here, headed—

"THE HUSBAND OF BELLE BOYD.—The husband of Belle Boyd, the famous Rebel Spy, took refreshments in the guard-house of the Citizen's Volunteer Hospital on Friday afternoon, on his way to Fort Delaware. Dr. (?) Kenderdine was *careful to provide secure quarters for this noted individual.*"

Jan. 9th and 10th.—Damp weather. Afflicted with the "blues." My feet so swollen that I cannot put my boots on.

Jan. 11th.—Whitewashed our division to-day. The guard kept us out in the snow, that had fallen heavily. Passed the time away by snow-balling one another. One of these frozen missiles falling near a sentry, he deliberately fired upon us, but fortunately without doing any mischief, although the ball ploughed the snow up very near one of our party.

CHAPTER XIV.

The " Pens "—Officers' Barracks—Privates' Barracks—The "Galvanized" Barracks—Galvanization and its results—General T.'s experiment—The Barracks by Night—A Reckless Sentry—The wrong Man shot.

THE places where the prisoners are held here are called " pens;" and they are correctly designated, for they are nothing more. Any one who may at any period of his life have attended a " cattle-show" can readily portray to himself the places we inhabit. These habitations, boarded and roughly put together, remind one very forcibly of old-fashioned farm-house barns, where, in the old times, your poor horse shivered the night through, standing uneasily in his stall, whilst his master slept comfortably within the chimney-corner. Officially and by courtesy they were denominated "barracks," of which there are three distinct kinds upon this island; viz., the Officers' Barracks, the Privates' Barracks, and last, but not least, the Allegiance Barracks; or, as they are commonly termed, the "Whitewashed," or "Galvanized Barracks."

In the Officers' Barracks are held some fifteen or eighteen hundred officers and political prisoners—about 150 in all of the latter.

In the Privates' Barracks, which occupy a little more space, and whose divisions are somewhat larger than those of the former, are crowded together, in their misery, some nine or ten thousand soldiers, from almost every regiment and command in the Southern Confederacy. Many of these poor fellows are but half-clad, and suffer terribly from the cold, inclement winter of the North. Many of them, by far the largest portion, are without friends in the North to whom they could apply, and are therefore indebted to the Yankees for the very little clothing that is at times given to them, but which is never given unless every vestige of the original garment has entirely disappeared, and common decency demands it. Many of them are young, scions of some of the noblest and proudest families in the South; men who before this war knew naught of want and trouble; men who had from infancy been reared in the lap of luxury, and are now enduring everything — insult, imprisonment, and starvation—willingly, and without murmuring; patriots, whose names will yet live to be handed down to posterity as noblest among the noble.

And, lastly, the Galvanized Barracks. These are domiciled by Southern soldiers who have taken the oath of allegiance to the United States upon being imprisoned here. These "patriots" remain in this delectable spot for one year, and are made to work for the State, to prove their devotion to Mr. Lincoln's Government, by hauling wood and doing the disagreeable duties of the prison. These fellows are allowed to draw rations daily, and to live the same as the garrison in every respect as regards their food. Moreover, they are permitted to receive boxes containing clothing and luxuries, which those who choose to remain constant to their principles cannot, unless they possess the influence of outside friends.

As regards their love for the " old flag," and devotion to the Union, I can hardly deem myself competent to pronounce judgment correctly. But an excellent story is told of these individuals, which is not unworthy of attention, as it may in a measure serve to show how far these *patriots* should be trusted.

General S—— and his staff once paid them a visit. Upon entering their abode, the General stated to them that there was to be an exchange of prisoners, and that all those who still desired to go back to the South might do so.

"Now," he added, "all those who feel inclined to do so, step over on the left of the division."

Every one of them went over; not a man remaining of the many who had grown to love the Federal Government as at present conducted.

It is said General S—— laughed, and remarked, "Well, that will do; I only wanted to find out whom I could trust—to ascertain if any of you were really sincere."

These barracks or pens are divided into divisions, each division having a stove, for the purpose of heating, in a manner, quarters that would otherwise be untenable. They range in length from eighty to one hundred feet, and in breadth measure about thirty feet. They are separated from one another by thin partitions of boarding, so that really they are quite connected, as conversations carried on in one can be distinctly heard in the other. On each side of these places, wide structures of wood are built, two stories in height, which are reached by means of wooden chats nailed to the supports. Upon these elevated platforms each prisoner is apportioned off so much space for his sleeping and cooking purposes.

At night calcium lights, placed at one end of the barracks, throw their broad glare upon the square of something less than an acre of mud and boards. Delectable spot in rainy weather, with its ditches filled with muddy yellow water! Splendid place in the summer for disease; and many a poor fellow has looked his last upon this earth, dying here, far away from his home, struck down by the small-pox or some virulent, fearful malady.

Escapes during the summer months are not unfrequent; but in winter all such attempts are put an end to from the inclemency of the weather, the floating ice in the river, and the utter impossibility of any one, however bold and daring a swimmer he might be, living any length of time in the water.

The regulations for the prevention of escape, &c., are rigorous enough, but they are still more rigorously carried out.

One of the prisoners in the Privates' Barracks, rising one morning, carelessly, and without thinking of the consequences that might ensue, threw some dirty water out of the pigeon-hole which answered the purpose of a window, and served to lighten up in a manner the gloom within.

The water, splashing on the ground, attracted the attention of a sentinel who was standing guard about twenty paces distant; and, without warning, he brought his musket to a "ready," and fired haphazard in the direction from whence the water was thrown, hitting, not the aggressor, but an innocent youth who had just awakened, and was gazing out upon the dreary scene that presented itself before him, perfectly unconscious of his danger, or how near unto death's door he was passing.

CHAPTER XV.

A piteous Spectacle—The Old Men's Petition—Piety of the Southern Soldiery—A Young Men's Christian Association—A Prison Service—Our Guardians—Colonel Wood—Mr. Wilson—Tom S. the Toady—How Tom got his Situation—The Ladies' Attendants—Aunt Lizzie—Mr. L.—The Spy Discomfited—Our Cuisine—Scrap Pudding—How the Prison Officers made their Profit.

ABOUT the middle of January I saw one of the most piteous spectacles, I think, that I ever had the misfortune to witness. Four men, old and decrepit, one of them tottering on the entrance to the valley of shadows, men whose gray beards and venerable aspects ought to have commanded at least sympathy from the presiding powers at Washington, were brought in as prisoners. They were to be held here until exchanged —men who could not possibly be of any benefit whatever to either side, North or South. These men were arrested on the 3rd of August last by a captain in the United States navy, who was on shore, in command of a raiding-party, and who brought them back prisoners on board his vessel. They were confined in the hold for five months, and then transferred to the supply steamer *Massachusetts*, and sent to Philadelphia, and from thence, upon her arrival, were forwarded to Fort Delaware. Truly if this was the sole result of the brave captain's raid, he had nothing to feel proud of.

Upon their arrival here they excited the "commiseration" even of Adjutant Ahl, who informed them, if they would take the oath and draw up a petition to the Secretary of War, that he himself would forward it for them to the proper authorities. Below I subjoin the letter that they had written, by friends who volunteered their services in the barracks, and to which they respectively signed their names. One of them recounted to me his misfortunes and those of his comrades, and I confess that, as I sat listening to his recital, I felt moved. "We have been treated very badly, very badly," he said, in conclusion—"confined in the hold of the vessel for most of the time; and we are all of us very old men, sir, and we never did them any harm."

"Jan. 16th, 1865.
"Capt. Geo. H. Ahl, A.A.A. Genl.
"Sir,

"In accordance with your request, we enclose you the written petition to the Secretary of War, and we solicit your kindness to have it forwarded at your earliest convenience. You have seen our condition, and can appreciate the truthfulness of our statements. If, therefore, you find it consistent with your views of duty and humanity to add thereto the recommendation of the Commanding General of this post, or such other good word in our behalf as you may deem best, you will add greatly to the obligations we are already under for your considerate attention.

"The Petitioners."

PETITION.

"Jan. 16th, 1865.
"Hon. E. M. Stanton, Secretary of War.
"Sir,

"The Petition of the undersigned humbly sheweth, that they are citizens of the State of Georgia, and residents of McIntosh County, whence we were seized and taken on the 3rd of August last, by a raiding-party under the command of Captain Colverconerris, of the United States Navy, and, after five months of close and severe confinement on board vessel, have been transferred to the military prison at Fort Delaware, where we are at the present writing of this. We were, at the time of our capture, peaceable citizens, engaged in the pursuit of our several civil occupations, non-combatants, having never been engaged in any military service or duty to the Confederate authorities, and are, from our advanced age and physical disabilities, wholly incapable of such service as the field, neither of us being less than fifty, some of us over sixty years of age, and one of us being deprived of a leg, which was lost by accident many years ago. Being thus incapable of contributing anything towards the continuance of this war, or the result of this unfortunate struggle between the sections of our once common country, and having, in the course of nature, but few remaining days to look for on this earth, we indulge the hope, and appeal to the humanity of the enlightened Government in whose hands we are placed, that those days shall not be shortened by the terrific rigours of an imprisonment which cannot otherwise be endured. To this appeal of our extreme age and helplessness, and our entirely civil and non-combative character, we have to add that our homes are now within your military lines as recently established by the forces under the command of Major-General Sherman. Under this state of affairs, we humbly beg to be, as soon as practicable, released from confinement and returned to our homes, where we engage to remain as heretofore, and, as our physical condition compels, quiet and peaceable citizens. To this end we are willing and ready to subscribe to the usual oath of allegiance to the United States Government. Trusting that the petition and appeal may receive a speedy and favourable response, we shall, as in duty bound,

"Ever remain, your obedient Servants,
"WM. JAMES CANNON,
" CHARLES LINGOAUT,
" WM. RILY TOWNSEND,
" WM. SOMERLIN."

Yankees generally are very susceptible to flattery, at least those in authority at Washington; and let us hope that the few masterly touches of the ingenious, if not diplomatic author, will not fail to have its desired effect upon hearts that are proverbial for their adamantine qualities. Since my sojourn here I have had ample opportunities of observing the spirit of piety and godliness amongst the Southern soldiery. A Young Men's Christian Association was organized some time ago, and prayer meetings are held nightly in some one of the divisions, whilst prayers and readings from the Bible take place in each division every evening about half an hour before the lights are put out, either conducted by some chaplain or Confederate officer.

In their pious regard for the Sabbath day and God's command to keep it holy, I know of no nation which approaches nearer to the marked devotion of the English people than the Southerners. The Sabbath day is always passed in a quiet and orderly manner, service being held in different parts of the barracks. It was my very good fortune to attend the meeting held by the Rev. Mr. Kinsolving, in Division 23. His service was attended by all grades of rank, and he certainly spoke and read with

—what is very rare with the public speakers of the present day — much feeling and pathos, so different from the rant and fume of a certain sensational preacher of the word of God that I once had the misfortune to hear in the "City of Churches."*

You will like to hear something of our gaolers. Here they are. Colonel Wood, our superintendent, could be a gentleman if he wished. With a mind cultured and at once deep and penetrating, he appears to have brutalized himself by contact with those with whom he has associated. I have watched the man closely in both phases— in one, running about the ground like an enraged tiger, whilst his subordinates clear to the right and left, fearful of their tyrannical master. Finally venting his spleen

* Brooklyn, Long Island, State of New York.

upon some unfortunate one, he subsides into quiet, and his official dignity now feels half-ashamed of the disturbance he has succeeded in creating about him!

I have heard him use language that modest ears would hardly dare to listen to—not merely commonplace oaths, but curses both loud and deep, and horrible to hear. A fit disciple of Tom Payne and Voltaire! for W. is an Atheist.

Atheism is his hobby. His arguments are good in the defence of his "creed;" but, reasoner, and a deep one, though he is, I do not believe that he has faith in it. Conversing on this subject one day he said, "There is my Bible," laying his hand on a volume of Voltaire!

"And, Colonel Wood," I replied, "like Voltaire, on your death-bed you will cry out, in your agony, upon God to save you!"

He pondered for a moment, then said, "Well, I might. Your Bible says, that those who believe in Christ, even in the eleventh hour, shall be saved."

Again, the Colonel can be as suave and polite, as affable and courteous, as any who have moved in the best society—as gentle and as tender. It is only, Madame Rumour whispers, that he is cruel when under the influence of morphia or opium. In his movements he is quick and energetic—a man of medium stature. His is a peculiar eye—keen and gray; at times cold and perfectly expressionless, at others full of shrewdness and keenness. Dressed in black coat and gray trousers and vest, his large head covered with a broad-brimmed black slouched hat, you have W. P. Wood, the Vidocq, or, better still, perhaps the Jonathan Wild, of America.

Mr. Wilson, the Colonel's right-hand man, the under-superintendent, from what little I saw of him, appeared to be a gentleman, straightforward in his dealings, and a man of very few words. He dresses plainly, and wears a slouched felt hat. Every one wears felt hats now. " It is only foreigners and Southerners who carry canes and wear tall hats," said a friend of mine to me one day when in conversation with him.

Next to the Colonel, W. is the busiest man in the prison. He it is who has charge of the prisoners, and who rules supreme in the Colonel's absence. Every morning at eight o'clock he comes round and calls the muster-roll of the prisoners in their rooms, and hands them their letters, which, however, are invariably opened and read before they leave the office below.

Colonel Colby, the military commandant,

who has charge of this post, I saw but little of; but we all liked him, for he was ever courteous and polite, and had always a good word for us.

Fortunately for myself, I was not under the tender guardianship of the "officers of the Keyes," so of them I can say but little, save that they attended to their business with punctilious strictness.

Another individual in this modern Bastille is a decided toady to Colonel Wood. He rejoices in the name of Tom Stackpole, and has charge of the beds and bedding, and he attempts to imitate him in his every action. In his accomplishment of swearing he is even a greater proficient than the Colonel. In his walk he outdoes him. If there is a man that he hates and fears more than all others, it is certainly Colonel Wood. Indeed, I think, like

Jonathan Wild, the Colonel can trust his menials because he knows a portion of their life which it would not do to publish to the world.

During the late election in the United States, Tom made himself conspicuous by pulling down from the pole upon which it was hoisted the American flag, and tearing it because it bore upon its folds the names of McClellan and Pendleton. For this hardy act he was promoted to the position that he now occupies.

The female servants of the prison, with the exception of "Aunt Lizzie," were the worst and most degraded beings I ever had the misfortune of seeing. The Five Points of New York, or the lowest dens of infamy, could not produce a worse crowd. Yet this scum were hired to wait upon the ladies who were here held—for

Heaven knows what; but prisoners nevertheless.

But "Aunt Lizzie," as she was called by every one here, stood on her dignity. No one insulted her; always laughing and good natured, Aunt Lizzie prided herself upon belonging formerly to the Snowdon family. "My name, sah, am Aunt Lizzie Snowdon, sah, and I'm berry proud of it, sah." Straightforward and ever scrupulous, in her Colonel Wood had one faithful attendant. She was not to be bribed nor cajoled. None could see her smiling face and feel gloomy: a good word she had for everybody. She it was who mended our linen and washed our clothes. Aunt Lizzie was certainly a good feature in this prison, and many besides myself will, I am sure, remember her with feelings of gratitude.

Mr. L—— is another gentleman who

rejoices in belonging to the corps that is commanded by Colonel Wood. He is the "Jerry Sneak" of this institution. His nose is everywhere, and his eyes are upon everything. If a visitor comes to see a friend confined here, Mr. L―― stands near at hand, noting down in his memory the conversation, whilst apparently engaged in trimming his nails, or fixing his eyes on dreamland, as he notes down their words. If in the court when the prisoners are walking about, he is always looking on and smiling, or has some soft word of "endearment" to say to new-comers, to bring against them when their time comes. I was particularly the object of his hatred, and our hate was mutual.

I had very grievously offended him. One day a gentleman called to see me. Upon entering I seated myself close to the gentleman. Mr. L—— took a chair, and, placing his legs between us, stretched himself complacently at full length, and prepared, as was his custom, to listen.

Of course our hopes of a conversation were to all appearances at an end. For some moments I stood it calmly, but at last I could stand it no longer. "There are," I said very quietly, "in this prison, spies; bearers of stories, ever ready for anything mean and contemptible; but the meanest and most contemptible of them all is — I beg your pardon, sir," turning suddenly to him, "is yourself, Mr. L——."

"I can't help it," said that individual, looking piteously at me. But the shot had taken effect, Mr. L—— removed his chair to the fire, and our conversation was uninterrupted.

Of the *cuisine* of Fort Delaware there is not much to be said in praise. Two meals are served out to us daily, consisting of one piece of peculiarly constructed bread, and one ditto of indescribable salt, yellowish-coloured pork, or meat that has had its nutriment entirely boiled out of it in the making of soup for the garrison, previous to its being apportioned out to the prisoners.

Occasionally a mixture, designated by our persecutors as soup, and containing an ample sufficiency of maggots, is doled out to us in tin pots. It is an indescribable *olla prodrida* of soups of every kind, and in its appearance reminds one irresistibly of the sty and the trough. Coffee and tea are luxuries never seen in the shed where we receive our rations. Only those who are fortunate enough to have money are ever enabled to procure these articles from the sutler, who, although selling a very good kind, does not forget to charge a very exorbitant price for his considerate (!) kindness.

These meals thus served out to us are called respectively breakfast and dinner, misnomers for such luxuries in the outside world, however poor they may be. What would our English friends, who are, I believe, by no means averse to good cheer, think, if they could try it for a few weeks, of the nutritious food, the unparalleled good treatment of the prisoners held here, of which the Federals boast so loudly?

These pleasant meals are served to us at nine in the morning and three in the afternoon. The cook-house, as it is named, from whence this food is served out to us by its grinning demons, is a large room, in length about one hundred feet, by sixty in width, filled partially with long and very narrow tables, constructed of pine-boards. Upon two generally, though sometimes there were more, are placed at regular intervals our pieces of bread (by courtesy) and our ditto of meat. About half-past eight some subordinate of the cook-house shouts out the command to " fall in 28!" or " 31!" and whichever portion of the officers' barracks may be first mentioned, the inmates immediately respond by coming forth from their separate divisions, and falling in by twos or threes, march up to the entrance of the cook-house.

Here we are generally kept waiting for several minutes until the door is thrown open, when we enter and file in single column down the table, taking our allotted rations as we pass on, until the end of the table is reached, when on again, we face to the right about, retracing our steps out of the room, and are once more fain to return to our dens or eat in the open air. The latter alternative, however, is not very often chosen, as it is winter, and we are but scantily clothed.

Each division, during the cold weather, is provided with a stove for the purpose of heating, in a measure, places that would have otherwise been untenantable. Over this some one or more of us are generally pretty much occupied in cooking sundry nondescript dishes, composed of odds and ends, and which I find from experience are not altogether unsavoury after once conquering the repugnance felt upon being brought into contact with such very unaccustomed food. Coffee-pots, tea-pots, and oftentimes mugs and dippers, are piled upon every conceivable spot or space large enough to admit of such packing; and in cold weather to approach anywhere near the stove is a thing utterly impossible, owing to the numbers surrounding it.

Political prisoners have the privilege of procuring their meals from the kitchen, provided they can make some arrangement with the heads of that department, and have the money necessary to back them in such arrangements. After I had been imprisoned for two weeks, I managed to have "an interview" with the presiding dignitary of this steaming sanctum, which resulted favourably; and henceforth, instead of living, as I had for the past fourteen days, upon bread and water (for I never ate the pork), I dined regularly upon meat, potatoes, and coffee for breakfast, dinner, and supper, having for my comrade and messmate Major R——, Quartermaster on General Ramseur's staff.

Several messes of this description were thus formed, many of them having from six to eight members. By feeing the "cookmaster" we managed to get several extras occasionally, so that, altogether, we managed to get along better than we should have done had we been without money or without friends.

For a consideration, some one of the lower class of men confined here enacts the duties of cook, and sets and clears off the dishes (tin-ware) from the table (in our case a cheese-box on legs), and announces the meals when ready for us. We might have fared better, but Rumour whispers that the sutler and presiding officials at the fort are leagued together, and that the order prohibiting luxuries being forwarded here by friends was made as much for the benefit of themselves as for the irritation that it occasioned to us, as it is utterly impossible to procure anything unless through the shark of a sutler, who charges exorbitantly for his politeness.

CHAPTER XVI.

Miss McDonough—A brutal Outrage—Treatment of Mr. W. R. Coyner—The "Court-martial"—Sentence—"Tossing in a Blanket"—The Torture by Fire—Fort Delaware—A Box of Clothing—A Man of Consequence—Adjutant and General—The Blankets at last—The "Softest Plank."

I HAVE already spoken of poor Miss McDonough. She was taken prisoner last summer upon the charge of having murdered a Federal officer. At the time of this alleged murder, Miss McDonough was nowhere in the vicinity, and it was only in hopes that her brother would be advised of her arrest, and surrender himself in her stead, that this shameful seizure was made.

James McDonough was a Lieutenant in Mosby's command, somewhere in the Valley of the Shenandoah, and Captain B. was shot by him (not murdered) when, during a skirmish, he refused to surrender himself prisoner. It was for this justifiable act of war she was made to suffer. Miss McDonough was compelled to remain in a room* perfectly stifling with noisome smells. Add to this the fact that she was continually fretting for fear her brother would deliver himself up for her. Can it then be wondered at that she should have died there, far away from her friends and those she loved?

* The same in which Belle Boyd was held so long.

During my sojourn in the Carroll Prison, I one evening called upon Mrs. ——, a lady prisoner from Galveston, Texas, who tended Miss McDonough with motherly care during her illness. Poor Mollie was then in a state of semi-insensibility, and was barely conscious of what was going on about her, when Colonel Wood, the superintendent of the prison, burst into the room, shouting out at the top of his voice, "Hooray! Jem McDonough's caught, and will swing, by——! before the week is out."

Miss McDonough slowly raised herself in the bed until nearly upright, stared wildly about her for an instant, and, uttering a piercing shrink, fell insensible upon the floor.

I sprang forward, but Mrs. —— was beside her before me; and I, turning full upon the author of this outrage, remarked excitedly, " By ——! Colonel Wood, if I ever catch you in Virginia when I get a command, you shall swing for this, sir."

Another instance of Yankee brutality and vindictiveness was related to me by the young gentleman himself, Mr. R. Coyner, a private in the old 7th Virginia regiment of cavalry.

At the time of his capture he was on furlough at Moorfields, Virginia. On the 12th of October, 1863, he was taken prisoner by a force of Federal infantry, under Captain Jarbon, and conveyed to Petersburg, Western Virginia, when he was handed over to Colonel Mulligan, who not only paroled him, but treated him with kindness and attention.

Here he remained until the 24th of October, when he was sent under a strong guard to New Creek Station, on the Baltimore and Ohio Railroad, where he arrived late at night on the 25th. Here his sufferings began. He was thrown into a large damp cellar, where were huddled together about seventy Yankee deserters, murderers, and bounty pumpers, where he was kept until the 26th, subsisting upon hard biscuits and cold water, which were served to them twice during the day.

On the 26th he was taken from thence and carried to Baltimore. Upon his arrival he was placed in Campbell's slave-pen, then under the charge of the infamous Colonel Fish, who was afterwards sentenced to the Albany Penitentiary for various crimes. Early on the morning of the 27th, Mr. Coyner was again ordered out of his place of confinement, and conducted, still under guard, to Fort McHenry, which he reached about 11 a.m. of the same day, and was immediately placed in what is known as the "Solitary Cell."

Here the company was as select as that at New Creek Station, comprising as it did murderers, and thieves, and other wretches of the deepest dye. In this solitary cell, where he was doomed to pass a weary interval of time, no windows admitted the light of day, no lamp was permitted at night. The apartment, or rather den, was cold and noisome; its walls thick with mildew, the floor covered with filth of every kind, and literally swarming with insects; none of the prisoners held here being ever allowed to leave the place for any purpose whatever.

Here young Coyner upon entering found two other Confederate soldiers with ball and chain attached to their legs; the cause assigned for this treatment by the Yankee authorities being simply, that they were *Confederates.*

Young Coyner himself had not remained here more than an hour when the sergeant entered, and with the assistance of his men placed a 42 Por. ball and chain upon his left ankle, adding that if he attempted to take it off he would shoot him. He remained here, and in this condition, for three months and a half, and his sufferings, as he related them to me, were certainly horrible in the extreme.

The first night that he passed in this "hell upon earth," as he termed it, could never be obliterated from his memory. A mock court-martial was held, before which he was arraigned upon the charge of being a rebel and guerilla; the remainder of those in the den looking on, laughing spectators of the scene.

Of course the result of this court-martial may be inferred; he was found guilty, and the court pronounced the following sentence upon him; viz., "To be tossed in a blanket *until lifeless.*" This was immediately carried into effect, the Federal guards looking on, amused spectators of the scene, taking no heed of his piteous appeals to them for mercy or protection, but on the contrary inciting his persecutors by words and gestures to carry the sentence into effect.

Handed over to them, he was tossed thirteen times, each time falling heavily upon his head or sides; when, finally, more dead than alive, he was permitted to crawl off amidst the jeers and laughter of his tormentors, who were highly elated at the manner in which they had eventually succeeded in eliciting groans from their unfortunate martyr.

Thoroughly sick, and feeling like one more dead than alive, poor Coyner, bruised and sore, endeavoured to court sleep, and thus, in a measure, to drive off the fearful thoughts that were at times nearly driving him mad. He eventually fell into an uneasy slumber, and may have slept for an hour, when he was awakened by fire being applied to his feet by the "Judge-Advocate," of this mock court, who gloried in the name of Kelly, and who exultantly boasted of having murdered his captain for greenbacks.

This fresh torture of young Coyner was considered the very acme of pleasure and amusement by his tormentors, some of whom held him, whilst others applied the burning paper to his feet, the fire being supplied to them for this purpose by the sentries. He showed me the scars caused by the severe burns that he had received— scars that he will take with him to the grave.

It was in vain that he appealed for mercy. At last, wearied out, they permitted him to go free for the time being. "By these miserable brutes," said young Coyner, "I was not permitted to speak in defence of my country, nor yet assert my rights. If I remonstrated with them, I was knocked down and kicked by my brutal persecutors, oftener beaten.

"This kind of treatment I endured for a period of three months and a half, when I was ordered out of this horrible place by the Provost-Marshal, whom I found to be kind and compassionate, and who in my case was but obeying his superiors. He placed me in a very nice and comfortable room which the Confederate officers held, and removed from my ancle the ball and chain that had so long been my companions in my misery.

"Here I remained until the 12th of May, when I was removed to Fort Delaware to serve out a sentence of court-martial; viz., 'Hard labour for the war'—that had been passed upon me by my tyrannical captors."

It is worthy of remark that, out of those nine officers who composed one of the most atrocious military commissions that was ever assembled, and before whom he was arraigned, all, with the exception of one of its members, have already met a violent death. Eight were killed before the 20th of June by Southern bullets, and the remaining one lies already at the point of death, struck down by consumption's fatal shaft, which is slowly but surely working out his fate.

"Here I am for the present," he said, in concluding his narrative: "how long I am to remain I know not; but I am willing to suffer any and every thing for my country and her cause."

Previous to my incarceration in Fort Delaware, and whilst I was yet a prisoner in the Carroll, I received a letter from my mother, in which she mentioned that she was about to forward to me a trunk filled with winter clothing and some few little articles necessary for my comfort, but before it came I was sent to the fort.

Here the *régime* was much stricter, and prohibited the prisoners from receiving anything whatsoever in the shape of food, and it was only by special permit that even clothing was allowed to be sent here, the different expresses refusing to accept parcels unless they had pasted upon the outside the passport of the fort.

Desirous of keeping myself warm at least, I wrote to the Assistant Adjutant-General of the post, George W. Ahl, the following letter:—

"Jan. 4th, 1865,
"Officers' Barracks,
"Fort Delaware.
"Capt. Geo. W. Ahl.
"Sir,—" Will you permit the undersigned to receive two bl..nkets and a box that has already been forwarded to him from his mother's residence, Brooklyn, Long Island?
"And I am, Sir,
"Respectfully,
"S. Wilde Hardinge."

This I forwarded to him by mail, although my friends scouted the idea of my ever receiving an answer to it; and their conjectures were correct, for Captain Ahl did not deign to notice it. Whether it was owing to the weight of his official duties, or to his supreme contempt for rebels, I was never able to ascertain.

Finally, however, one day, as I sat thinking upon my dreary imprisonment, of you my wife, and home associations, affected decidedly with the "blues,"—Mr. J., whose misfortune it was to have been a Democrat and the editor of a Baltimore journal, said, "Well, Mr. H., have you received a reply to the letter you wrote the other day?"

"No, sir," I responded, gloomily.

"Well, try the General: he ranks several grades above an adjutant, and is therefore not so important as the lesser bird."

"By Jove!" I replied, "the idea is a good one;" and forthwith I wrote.

Certes, the General was far more

polite and attentive to his prisoners than his adjutant; for the next day I received by mail the following order:—

☞ Paste on the outside of the Box.
☞ Anything not mentioned in this Permit will be Confiscated.

Head-quarters,
Fort Delaware,
Jan. 10th, 1865.

Mr.
　Supt. Old Carroll Prison,
　　Has permission to send:

(1) One box now in his possession, provided it contains clothing,

　To Sam W. Hardinge,
　　Political Prisoner,
A Prisoner of War at this Fort.

By command of
Brig.-General A. Schoepf,
G. W. Ahl,
Capt. & A.A.A. Genl.,
P. S. Hemings.

Of course this was all that was desired; and in a few days I had the extreme pleasure of overhauling the contents of this much-coveted box. And, oh! you of the outside world, who have never in winter slept without blankets, nor indulged in that very dubious luxury "the softest plank," for a bed in some modern bastile— you, I say, can never conceive the joy that I felt swelling up within me as "I laid me down to sleep" that night, wrapping myself up in this warm embrace. You, doubtless, would not envy me the luxury; and yet there were plenty of poor fellows here, without money and without friends, sleeping calmly and peacefully around me, as I have slept, without blankets to cover them, only their "martial cloaks"—and they are very ragged—for a covering.

CHAPTER XVII.

Wanted at the Fort—The Order for Release—Farewells—Free at last—A cool Reception—An undignified Costume—No Conveyance—The Walk to Wilmington—Home once more—Conclusion of Mr. Hardinge's Journal.

On the 3rd of February, whilst seated with Major R. and Adjutant C——, talking of our anticipated exchange, the sergeant of the barracks came into the division and inquired for me. I immediately descended from my perch and presented myself before him, inquiring as I did so the purport of his visit.

"You're wanted at the fort—General P—— wants you. Follow me," was the reply.

Half wondering what it was, and drawing closer about me my apology for a blanket, for it was a very cold afternoon, I followed my conductor until I reached the fort, when I was immediately ushered into the august presence of the commandant, who stared hard at me, without, however, saying anything.

One of his aides, evidently a secretary, handed me, after a few moments had elapsed, the following document, which was to be my safe-conduct by sea and land:—

"Special Orders:
    "No. 62.   "Head-quarters,
                       "Fort Delaware, Del.,
                            "Feb. 3d, 1865.
"S. Wilde Hardinge (Political Prisoner) is hereby released from confinement at this Post, in compliance

with the following Telegram from the War Department, dated Feb. 3d, 1865 :—

"Brig.-Genl. A. Schoepf,
      "Fort Delaware.

"The Secretary of War directs the release of S. Wilde Hardinge, a Prisoner at Fort Delaware. Acknowledge receipt, and inform me when Mr. Hardinge leaves the island.

(Sgd.)   "JAMES A. HARDEE,
         "Col. and Insp.-Genl. ;
(Seal)   "A. SCHOEPF,
         "Brig.-Genl. Comg."

The General then remarked, "Mr. H——, you have now our permission to leave the island. Will you go to-night or to-morrow morning? Do you go to Baltimore or New York City? I presume you will leave for Europe by the *first steamer?*"

To this I made answer, saying, "I will go now. My destination is New York; and I thank God I am free. Rest assured that I shall not trouble the Government by remaining longer than I can help. Good afternoon, sir;" and, turning, I left the room and walked rapidly back, still accompanied by the sergeant, to the barracks, that soldier remarking, " By ——! you're an awfully lucky chap."

I was not long, I can assure you, in packing up what few things I had; and then came the final adieus and partings. I confess that I felt badly as I took Major R—— by the hand and bade him good-bye, for he had ever been a good friend and counsellor of mine.

I am not ashamed to confess that my eyes were filled with tears as one after another of my friends gathered around, shaking hands with me, wishing me a " God speed you, Hardinge," " God bless you, my boy," " Hope to meet you in

Dixie soon," "Write to me," &c.—words that I shall never forget, for they came from the lips of some of the bravest spirits in the Southern Confederacy.

It was very fortunate that I had taken the precaution to hide my papers carefully about my person; for, upon re-entering the guard-room previous to leaving the island, my bundle was first thoroughly inspected, then my pockets, the lining of my felt hat, and my boots; but here the soldier employed for that purpose luckily stopped.

I was then permitted to step on board of a small steam-tug which lay at the wharf. This in a few moments cast off from her moorings, and she slowly glided away from the Château d'If of America, daintily picking her way through the miniature bergs that impeded our progress to the mainland, which, although only about seven miles distant, we were nearly two hours in reaching.

It was with feelings of unmistakable pleasure that I felt my feet pressing once more *terra firma*, and experienced the gratifying sensation awakening itself within me that I was once more my own master. So, drawing my tattered blanket about me, I stepped into the hotel that stood near the landing, and inquired the distance to Wilmington.

The proprietor of this country place eyed me suspiciously; the dog who had been basking at the fire rose and growled at me; and the frequenters of the place, who were seated round the stove smoking or drinking, by their looks inferred as plainly as tongue could speak, "He is an escaped prisoner." And no wonder, when I describe to you my presentation dress upon the occasion.

A felt hat, remarkable only for its being crownless, adorned my head; a ragged blanket sufficed—only in a measure, however—to keep the cold from my coatless body; a pair of " inexpressibles," horribly dilapidated, encased my lower extremities; a boot on one foot, and the other wrapped up in old rags. Is it a wonder, then, that I was an object of doubtful character?

Seating myself near the fire, I called for a glass of wine, which was handed to me by the bar-tender, who muttered something about a desire that he had of seeing "the colour of my money."

To this I replied by drawing out my pocket-book, and offering him a fifty-dollar greenback, desiring him to give me small moneys for it. In an instant the conduct of those present underwent a complete change; the bar-tender was all smirks and bows, and, with an urbanity that was all the more strikingly apparent from his former behaviour, desired to know if I wished to have an apartment.

"No; I wish to go to Wilmington. How far is it from here?"

"Sixteen miles," was the reply.

"Is there any conveyance that will take me there to-night?"

There was none.

"Hem! not if I will pay you well for it?"

"I wouldn't let a dog of mine go out this night," was the answer.

"Then I will walk," I said.

"Walk!" was chorussed simultaneously,

with astonishment depicted on their countenances.

"Yes, walk!" I reiterated, desperately.

"Well, if you get to Wilmington safely, you will do more than I expect you will, in that garb especially;" and the speaker looked at my costume with a sneer.

"Nevertheless, I am going," I said; and, suiting the action to the word, I rose, and, attended to the door of the hotel by the group of astonished villagers, I commenced the journey.

It had been snowing and raining alternately throughout the day, and the roads in this part of the country, never at any time when I saw them remarkable for their goodness, were ankle-deep with mud.

I shall never have the recollection of that night obliterated from my memory. Several times I was on the point of lying down on the road-side; but the love of life and the thought that—God willing—I should soon be at home, were strong within me, and I staggered on through the freezing rain and slushy snow.

Twice on the way I inquired at the door of a farm-house the direction that I was to take, and once the " gude wife " of the quiet homestead where I gained admittance prepared for me with her own white hands a cup of coffee, and pressed me to stay all night at her hospitable place—an invitation in which she was seconded by the rest of her family. Herself and husband were both English, and I shall not forget their kindness to me; and, when I at last rose to depart, the husband, wife, and children bade me a kind adieu, the husband accompanying me down the road some distance.

At last, just as the clock was striking ten, I staggered into the dépôt at Wilmington, just in time to catch the train for New York. I had accomplished the distance in four hours; but it was fully a week before I was able to walk or sit even with any degree of comfort.

Early in the morning I arrived in New York, and drove immediately to my brother's place of business. He was perfectly amazed at seeing me, and laughed immoderately at the deplorable figure I cut.

Eventually, having procured a suit of clothes, and enjoyed the luxury of a bath and the inexpressible feeling of delight that one feels in finding his body once more in contact with clean linen, I bade adieu to the United States, and started directly for the shores of hospitable and peaceful England.

CHAPTER XVIII.

Conclusion of Mrs. Hardinge's Narrative.

My memoirs were written, and a portion of them already in the hands of the publishers, when the startling news came which has thrilled all Europe and filled her inhabitants with horror—the assassination of Abraham Lincoln, President of the United States.

It was always the boast of Americans, were they Northern or Southern in their sentiments, that theirs was the only history that could show to the world a clear untarnished record of successful Republican rule. But their annals can be no longer so regarded; for, in the sudden demise of Mr. Lincoln by the bullet of an insensate fanatic, that peculiar institution of Europe, the school of the assassin, has transferred itself to the shores of America; and that country can no longer uphold her former boast that crime such as this had never been perpetrated under the Government commenced by George Washington.

Personally I had no animosity against the honourable gentleman who has wielded the sceptre of Northern power for four long years. His has been a trying position. No man probably in the pages of History took his seat under more inauspicious circumstances. The Press of the world warred furious warfare upon him. He was jeered and scoffed at; he was pronounced uncouth, vulgar, low, servile, and abject; disappointed politicians and opposition cliques vied with each other in calling him upon every occasion the "rail-splitter," and wiseacres of soothsaying proclivities speedily predicted that, with such a man as Abraham Lincoln at the head of the Government, the Union would most assuredly be split with as much precision and as quickly as Mr. Lincoln had been known to split rails when a backwoodsman in the Western wilds.

Although a member of Congress previous to his elevation to the presidential chair of all the United States not in rebellion, and having for his political opponent in his presidential campaign that great statesman, the late Mr. Douglas, Mr. Lincoln was not a forensic success.

His speeches and arguments, teeming with wit and dry humour, were better calculated to attract the backwoodsman, by whom he was looked upon as a leading man, than the riper and more mature intellects with which he was in after-days brought into contact.

I can appreciate and admire fully the character of such men who exemplify the sentence, "Out of nothing came something." As such I looked upon Lincoln, when, month after month, and then year after year, of his presidential term rolled by, and I saw how well he governed the Northern Republic and how firmly he held the reins of the Federal cause, which from time to time toppled upon the verge of a yawning chasm.

Now all is changed. Can any one believe that Mr. Johnson is the man who is to restore the Republic to what it was, save the nation from bankruptcy, and bring peace and good-will to America? It might not have been impossible with Mr. Lincoln; for that gentleman held out the olive-branch, concealing no deadly weapon beneath it, to General Lee and his little band of heroes. With Mr. Johnson at the head of the Government of the North, who can foresee anything save anarchy and dissolution? He will fiddle whilst Rome is burning.

Politically I did not like Mr. Lincoln, for in him I saw the destroyer. As long as it served his purpose, Mr. Lincoln boldly advocated the right of *Secession*. I trust that the accusation will not startle my readers; but such was the case; and I will cite one instance—when, as a representative, he openly avowed "that any nation or people in any portion of the world had a right to rise up and rebel against the mother-government if they wanted to."

When the North, in 1860-61, declared that she would usurp all rights, and have, whether or no the South wished it, and in direct violation of the Constitution, a strictly Northern president, Abraham Lincoln, still true to his former assertion of the right of Secession, accepted the nomination of the Chicago platform, and by this act inserted the wedge in that log called the *Union*. The log was ultimately split through force of circumstances.

There are those who maintain that in this world women have no right to interfere in the affairs of state, in politics, in plots and counter-plots. Others there are who, more chivalrous, are willing to admit that women have as much right to act, think, and speak as men. I do not set myself up as an advocate of the woman's right doctrine, but would rather appear in the character of a quiet lady expressing her sentiments, not so much to the public as to her immediate friends. Therefore I trust that the former class of gentlemen will here forgive what to them may appear presumption; especially as, in the preceding chapters of my book, I have endeavoured to avoid politics as much as possible.

But to return to my subject. The North boldly declared that she did not care much if the South did secede; and the South, never doubting the intentions of the North, took her at her word—seceded; and the consequence has been a civil war whose magnitude has never been surpassed, and whose slain can be counted, not by tens, but by hundreds of thousands.

Mr. Lincoln, as the representative of his nation, took the oath of office to uphold the Union "as it was." Then, after a while, "as it was" became "as it is." Finally, when Richmond fell and Lee surrendered, unwilling to be what Andy Johnson, "Beast" Butler, or "Jim" Lane of Kansas wanted him to be, a tyrant, he openly avowed his intention of effecting, if possible, a speedy union of North and South on the most conciliatory terms.

This was sufficient. He was from henceforth a doomed man; the sands of his life were numbered; and he slept, little dreaming of his danger, of the sword hanging above his head.

Not only was Lincoln doomed, but so

also were all those most in favour of conciliatory measures towards the South and her traders.

"The Constitution as it is," said the notorious "Senator Jim Lane," of Kansas, "is played out; and I am ready to see any man shot down who favours the Union as it was talked of by Mr. Lincoln." And on the evening of the very next day after Mr. Lincoln had favoured a conciliatory treatment towards the South he was shot down!

Englishmen! I appeal to your impartial judgment! I look to you for the discountenancing of the foul charge which Mr. Stanton has thrown upon the shoulders of our Southern leaders, that he might thereby induce the European Powers to withdraw their recognition of Southern belligerency. It is not the chivalrous sons of the South who have done this deed. The papers, indeed, make the assassin use the words "Sic semper tyrannis!" But if this be true, then, as a Virginian woman, I say, never was the State-motto of Virginia more unworthily abused.

And, in truth, our people have even more to regret in the death of President Lincoln than have the people of the North. When our noble old chieftain General Lee heard of the assassination, he covered his face, and refused to listen to the details of the murder; whilst, in the Libby Prison, where a large number of Southern soldiers were confined, the inmates on one of the floors held a meeting, and denounced the murder, passing resolutions that they were soldiers, and could not therefore applaud assassins.

Yet Mr. Secretary Stanton unblushingly charges the commission of this deed upon the South. There are those in the Northern States who will yet move heaven and earth to prove that it was the South; and to prove it money will be spent, bribes given, and, where money and bribes fail, threats will be used.

But I appeal to Europe to judge discriminately between North and South. Do not pronounce too hastily your judgment, nor cast upon a brave and chivalrous people the stigma of assassination.

Many have advised me to suppress these volumes, urging that their publication will probably cause my life-long banishment. But I cannot—I will not recede.

I firmly believe that in this fiery ordeal, in this suffering, misery, and woe, the

South is but undergoing a purification by fire and steel that will, in good time, and by God's decree, work out her own independence.

THE END

WILLIAM STEVENS, PRINTER, 37, BELL YARD, TEMPLE BAR.

Yet Mr. Secretary Stanton unblushingly charges the commission of this deed upon the South. There are those in the Northern States who will yet move heaven and earth to prove that it was the South; and to prove it money will be spent, bribes given, and, where money and bribes fail, threats will be used.

But I appeal to Europe to judge discriminately between North and South. Do not pronounce too hastily your judgment, nor cast upon a brave and chivalrous people the stigma of assassination.

Many have advised me to suppress these volumes, urging that their publication will probably cause my life-long banishment. But I cannot—I will not recede.

I firmly believe that in this fiery ordeal, in this suffering, misery, and woe, the

South is but undergoing a purification by fire and steel that will, in good time, and by God's decree, work out her own independence.

THE END